CATHOLIC HEROES OF
CIVIL AND HUMAN RIGHTS

MATTHEW DANIELS
ROXANNE KING

Catholic Heroes of Civil and Human Rights

1800s to the Present

IGNATIUS PRESS   SAN FRANCISCO

Cover collage by Enrique J. Aguilar

© 2024 by Ignatius Press, San Francisco
All rights reserved
ISBN 978-1-62164-677-8 (PB)
ISBN 978-1-64229-294-7 (eBook)
Library of Congress Control Number 2024936500
Printed in the United States of America ∞

CONTENTS

III
HOPE

IV
JUSTICE

V
CONSCIENCE

INTRODUCTION

As a young college student whose conscience was stirred by the social injustice she saw around her, Dorothy Day wondered where the saints were who would "try to change the social order, not just to minister to the slaves but to do away with slavery".[1] She became a journalist, found faith in Christ, and in 1933, the lowest point of the Great Depression, cofounded the *Catholic Worker* newspaper and movement to address poverty and oppression. For her social justice work, she is now called a Servant of God by the Catholic Church, the first step to being declared a saint.

Nicholas Black Elk was made famous through a book written about him and his boyhood vision that led to his vocation as a spiritual healer for his people. The book, *Black Elk Speaks*, ends just after the tragic 1890 Wounded Knee Massacre with a lament that the old ways were gone. Unfortunately, the book leaves out most of Black Elk's life. Black Elk was a convert to Catholicism who served as a catechist for decades. He was known among his people for bringing to them the good news about Jesus, whom the Lakota call Wanikiya, "he who makes live". Black Elk not only lived and shared a vibrant life of hope, but inspired hundreds to "walk the good red road", as he radiated "the healing love of *Wanikiya* into a broken world"[2] through his ministry.

---

[1] Dorothy Day, *The Long Loneliness: The Autobiography of Dorothy Day* (San Francisco: Harper & Row, 1952), 45.

[2] Damian Costello, "Nicholas Black Elk: Prophet to Lakota a Sign of Hope Today", *CatholicPhilly*, April 15, 2019, catholicphilly.com/2019/04/comment aries/nicholas-black-elk-prophet-to-lakota-a-sign-of-hope-today/.

Today this former medicine man is also called a Servant of God, on the way to being canonized.

When the famed 1961 Freedom Rides were in danger of ending because violent attacks in the Deep South led by segregationists and the Ku Klux Klan, Black student civil rights leader Diane Nash recruited fresh riders to continue the journey to desegregate interstate bus travel. Not even a request from Attorney General Robert Kennedy could dissuade her. Nash told Kennedy's assistant: "Sir, you should know, we all signed our last wills and testaments last night before they left. We know someone will be killed. But we cannot let violence overcome nonviolence."[3] The perseverance of Nash and her fellow students paid off: the Freedom Rides garnered a win for the civil rights movement when the Interstate Commerce Commission outlawed segregation in buses and bus terminals that fall.

These are glimpses of three of the sixteen Catholic heroes found in these pages: men and women from diverse backgrounds and eras, ranging from before Abraham Lincoln's Emancipation Proclamation to today's ongoing immigration crisis at the U.S.-Mexico border. They shared a commitment to live their Christian faith courageously. In doing so, they promoted the natural law pillars of freedom, perseverance, hope, justice, and conscience. They transformed "violence into love, sin into grace, hatred into forgiveness, and death into life".[4] They bore witness that through an authentic Christian, "light shines in the darkness, and the darkness

---

[3] Alex Mikulich, "A Last Will and Testament for Freedom", *National Catholic Reporter*, July 19, 2014, ncronline.org/news/people/last-will-and-testament-freedom.

[4] Bishop Donald Hying, "Understanding the Devotion to the Sacred Heart of Jesus and What It Means", *Simply Catholic*, accessed November 8, 2023, simplycatholic.com/why-the-sacred-heart/.

has not overcome it" (Jn 1:5). May they inspire you to be the light in this world God desires and to realize your own call to holiness.

I
FREEDOM

DEFINING FREEDOM

To almost everyone in the Western world, freedom—
liberty—stands at the heart of life. Wars are fought in the
name of freedom. The word is printed large on posters,
billboards, and bumper stickers. Countless songs have been
written about it. It is enshrined in the United States Declaration of Independence (man's "inalienable Rights" to
"Life, Liberty and the pursuit of Happiness") and in the
European Union Charter of Fundamental Rights ("Everyone has the right to liberty and security of person").[1] Freedom strikes us as sacred, unquestionable, a good in itself.
Yet do we know why freedom matters so much? Do we
even know what the word means?

Christians believe that freedom comes from God himself.
The opening chapter of the Bible tells us that God created
mankind in his own divine "image" (Gen 1:26), which does
not mean that he is some lifeless photograph. Rather, man
"participates in the light and power of the divine Spirit,"
as the *Catechism of the Catholic Church* explains (*CCC* 1704).
He shares in God's infinite life. Unlike all other creatures
on earth, man has a mind, reason, understanding, intelligence, and—most unique of all—a free will, the ability to
choose and to do (or not do) what, in his heart, he truly
believes to be good, not what some outside force imposes
on him (see *CCC* 1731). This inherent liberty shows how
much confidence God has in mankind, how much dignity

---

[1] Constitution of the United States, art. 1; European Union Charter of
Fundamental Rights, art. 6.

he sees in each person, like a proud father who entrusts his own children with responsibility for tasks around the house, even when he knows they might do them wrong—or not do them at all. Humans are not slaves to instinct (like wolves), slaves to society (like ants or bees), or even slaves to a predestined fate (like movie characters). God, who in Jesus Christ revealed mankind to be his beloved children, has raised us above that level. Pope Leo XIII called this liberty "the highest of natural endowments",[2] and the Second Vatican Council praised human freedom as "an outstanding manifestation of the divine image."[3] Man is free because God is absolutely free.

Of course, with this freedom comes the possibility of choosing evil, whether intentionally or not. Adam and Eve fell into this trap at the very beginning, when they listened to the serpent instead of their Creator. This "original sin" blurred the line between good and bad in the human mind, because it made them slaves to their own passions—such as fear, anxiety, or anger—rather than masters of them (see *CCC* 1739). It cast a deep shadow over all of history, where men, following in Adam's footsteps, have sought time and time again not only to take others' lives, but to deprive them of their God-given liberty, that "manifestation of the divine image." Think of Aztec civilization, where human sacrifice was as ordinary a part of religious practice as Mass is for Catholics today. Think of the centuries-long Atlantic slave trade, where basic human equality was categorically denied to a whole population of people—even by faithful Christians. Think of the Gulag Archipelago in twentieth-century Siberia, where those who dared criticize the So-

[2] Leo XIII, encyclical letter *Libertas* (June 20, 1888), no. 1.

[3] Second Vatican Council, Pastoral Constitution on the Church in the Modern World *Gaudium et Spes* (December 7, 1965), no. 17.

viet state were condemned to labor camps to freeze and starve.

Thus enters Jesus Christ, God incarnate. Like a "refiner's fire" (Mal 3:2), he comes to purify the human heart, charging it with a new power to do good through the Holy Spirit, so that it might bear fruit. The Savior goes out to "proclaim liberty to the captives" (Is 61:1), and those who believe in Christ participate in this divine mission in different ways. Clearly, society remains broken, to such an extent that even Saint Paul, who preached that "for freedom Christ has set us free" (Gal 5:1), did not think it was feasible to abolish the institution of slavery on this side of eternity (see Eph 6:5). Yet as the centuries rolled on and Christianity spread, the ancient practice of slavery—which was always opposed by the Catholic Church—did gradually dissolve, through the encouragement of such figures as Pope Gregory the Great.[4] The course changed suddenly, however, in the fifteenth century, when colonization in the New World created a massive hunger for cheap labor. European powers tapped into the African slave market and, through violence, greatly expanded it. From the outset, the Church spoke out strongly against this brutal slave trade, which was being practiced and endorsed by self-styled Christians.[5] Still, the practice continued for centuries, becoming a familiar bastion of European and American colonial life, and many Catholics took a stand against it.[6] While slavery was eventually

---

[4] "It is most fitting that men by the concession of manumission should restore to the freedom in which they were born those whom nature sent free into the world, but who have been condemned to the yoke of slavery by the law of nations." Gregory the Great, *Epistolae*, bk. 6, letter 12 (*PL* 77:803C–804A).

[5] Leo XIII, encyclical letter *In Plurimis* (May 5, 1888), nos. 16–17.

[6] See, e.g., Bartolomé de las Casas, *A Short Account of the Destruction of the Indies*, trans. Nigel Griffin (New York: Penguin, 1999).

abolished by the British Crown in 1834 and then by the United States in 1863, injustice lingered through both harsh laws and economic disenfranchisement. Here, too, many Catholics—some of whom had carried the yoke of slavery themselves—continued to join in the Savior's work of freeing the captive children of God, not primarily through political action, but through concrete love. In Part I, you will see just three stellar examples: Venerable Pierre Toussaint, Venerable Mother Mary Elizabeth Lange, and Patrick Cardinal O'Boyle.

The mission of freedom continues today. The *Catechism* affirms that "the right to the exercise of freedom . . . is an inalienable requirement of the dignity of the human person" (*CCC* 1738). Let us heed the call in our own way.

CHURCH DOCUMENTS
ON FREEDOM

from Pope John XXIII, *Pacem in Terris* (1963)

Any well-regulated and productive association of men in society demands the acceptance of one fundamental principle:
that each individual man is truly a person. His is a nature,
that is, endowed with intelligence and free will. As such he
has rights and duties, which together flow as a direct conse-
quence from his nature. These rights and duties are universal and inviolable, and therefore altogether inalienable. . . .

Pope Leo XIII declared that "true freedom, freedom worthy of the sons of God, is that freedom which most truly
safeguards the dignity of the human person. It is stronger
than any violence or injustice. Such is the freedom which
has always been desired by the Church, and which she holds
most dear. It is the sort of freedom which the Apostles res-
olutely claimed for themselves. The apologists defended it
in their writings; thousands of martyrs consecrated it with
their blood.". . .

The natural rights of which We have so far been speaking are inextricably bound up with as many duties, all apply-
ing to one and the same person. These rights and duties de-
rive their origin, their sustenance, and their indestructibility
from the natural law, which in conferring the one imposes
the other.

Thus, for example, the right to live involves the duty to
preserve one's life; the right to a decent standard of living,
the duty to live in a becoming fashion; the right to be free

to seek out the truth, the duty to devote oneself to an ever deeper and wider search for it.[1]

from Pope John Paul II, *Veritatis Splendor* (1993)

Human freedom and God's law are not in opposition; on the contrary, they appeal one to the other. The follower of Christ knows that his vocation is to freedom. "You were called to freedom, brethren" (Gal 5:13), proclaims the Apostle Paul with joy and pride. But he immediately adds: "Only do not use your freedom as an opportunity for the flesh, but through love be servants of one another."[2]

---

[1] John XXIII, encyclical letter *Pacem in Terris*, (April 11, 1963), vatican.va /content/john-xxiii/en/encyclicals/documents/hf_j-xxiii_enc_11041963_pace m.html.

[2] John Paul II, encyclical letter *Veritatis Splendor* (August 6, 1993), vati can.va/content/john-paul-ii/en/encyclicals/documents/hf_jp-ii_enc_0608199 3_veritatis-splendor.html.

PIERRE TOUSSAINT

From Slave to Philanthropist

Former slave and later wealthy entrepreneur and philanthropist Venerable Pierre Toussaint lived as a citizen of
heaven rather than of earth. Because he found dignity and
liberation in his Christian faith, which was the guiding light
of his life, he lived authentic freedom long before he was
freed under the law. "If ever a man was truly free, it was
Pierre Toussaint", declared Cardinal John O'Connor, who
opened Toussaint's cause for canonization in 1991.[1]

Born in the French colony Saint Domingue in 1766,
Pierre Toussaint was brought to the newly established United
States with other house slaves by his masters, Jean-Jacques
and Marie Bérard, in 1787.[2] The Bérards had fled their
Caribbean plantation during the rebellion that ultimately
brought an end to slavery in the French outpost and established Haiti as an independent nation.

In New York City, Toussaint, who wrote and spoke
French and had been trained to serve aristocracy, was ap-
prenticed to a hairdresser. Hugely successful at this new
craft, he saved the portion of his earnings that were his
to keep. Mr. Bérard, whose fortune was dwindling, died

---

[1] Cardinal John O'Connor, "In the Cathedral Crypt, A Prayer for Haiti",
Catholic New York, October 21, 1993, reprinted in Timothy Cardinal Dolan,
"To Whom Shall We Go?", *Timothy Cardinal Dolan*, August 25, 2010,
cardinaldolan.org/blog/to-whom-shall-we-go-13.

[2] Hannah Farnham Sawyer Lee, *Memoir of Pierre Toussaint: Born a Slave in
Santo Domingo* (Boston: Crosby, Nichols, and Company 1854), 2.

in 1801. When Mrs. Bérard could no longer pay the bills, Toussaint voluntarily supported her and the household from his hairdressing, in addition to carrying out his butler duties. This arrangement continued even after she remarried a struggling musician. In gratitude, she freed Toussaint as she neared death two days before Independence Day in 1807.[3] Although Toussaint was now a free man, slavery would not be outlawed in New York until 1827.

The industrious, charming Toussaint, who had become Manhattan's most popular hairdresser as well as the trusted confidant of his elite female clientele, saved for four years to purchase his sister Rosalie Toussaint's freedom, and that of his fiancée, fellow Haitian and New Yorker Juliette Gaston Noel.[4] As a free woman, Rosalie quickly married the man she loved in May 1811. Pierre and Juliette followed suit in August.

Prior to his marriage, Toussaint used his wealth, which he earned by working long hours daily (and later increased through investments) to help purchase the freedom of other slaves and to aid needy Haitian refugees. Risking his own health, he also cared for the sick during outbreaks of yellow fever and cholera. Friends sought his good counsel, and he comforted the grieving and incarcerated. He helped both Blacks and whites. "I have never felt I am a slave to any man or woman, but I am a servant of the Almighty God who made us all", Toussaint once told his sister. "When one of His children is in need, I am glad to be His slave."[5]

[3] Arthur Jones, *Pierre Toussaint: A Biography* (New York: Doubleday, 2003), 162.

[4] Ibid., 165.

[5] Tribunus, "Blessed Pierre Toussaint, the Voluntary Slave Who Confounded the Worldly", *Roman Christendom*, September 5, 2007, romanchris tendom.blogspot.com/2007/09/blessed-pierre-toussaint-voluntary.html.

After they got married, he and Juliette continued those charitable works. When Toussaint's sister Rosalie died, they adopted her infant daughter, Euphémie. They also took in orphaned Black youth, made sure they were educated, and helped them get jobs. Additionally, their home served as a refuge for travelers. Toussaint was the major fundraiser for Mother Seton's New York orphanage, and though he and his family worshiped at Saint Peter's Church, he raised money to build what is now Old Saint Patrick's Cathedral. He joined Juliette in financially supporting the Oblate Sisters of Providence, the first congregation of Black nuns. The couple were also benefactors of New York's first school for Black children.[6] At one point, noting Toussaint's wealth, a friend urged him to retire. Toussaint declined, saying, "I have enough for myself, but if I stop working I have not enough for others."[7]

A devout Catholic who attended daily Mass for sixty years, Toussaint was renowned for the Christian witness of his everyday life. Hannah Sawyer Lee, author of *Memoir of Pierre Toussaint, Born a Slave in Santo Domingo*, recounts that when a client was fishing for gossip, he told her, "Toussaint dresses hair, he is no news journal." When another sought to send a "disagreeable message" through him, he said, "I have no memory." Lee's sister was Toussaint's client and

[6] Jones, *Pierre Toussaint*, 175–76. See also Mary Maillard, "Pierre Toussaint and Marie-Rose Juliette Gaston", Black Past, blackpast.org/african -american-history/toussaint-pierre-and-juliette/; "Venerable Pierre Toussaint, 1766–1853", *United States Conference of Catholic Bishops*, accessed November 8, 2023, usccb.org/committees/african-american-affairs/road-sainthood -leaders-african-descent; "Venerable Pierre Toussaint", *Archdiocese of New York*, accessed November 8, 2023, archny.org/ministries-and-offices/cultural -diversity-apostolate/black-ministry/venerable-pierre-toussaint/; and "Venerable Pierre Toussaint, 1766–1853, Archdiocese of New York", *Catechist Cafe*, accessed November 8, 2023, catechistcafe.weebly.com/uploads/9/4/2/8/9428 334/saints_-_toussaint.pdf.
[7] Lee, *Memoir of Pierre Toussaint*, 25.

close friend Mary Anna Schuyler, whose journals served as
the basis for the biography. Lee writes: "He understood
the plain teachings of Christianity. He often quoted, in his
native language, from the Sermon on the Mount, and the
beatitudes seemed to have found their way to his heart."[8]

In carrying out the spiritual and corporal works of mercy,
Toussaint lived the beatitudes, the standard for Christian
perfection. Mary Anna Schuyler affectionately called him
"Saint Pierre",[9] and her husband, Philip Jeremiah Schuyler,
famously asserted, "I have met men who were Christians,
and men who were gentlemen, but I have only met one who
was both. And he was black."[10]

Toussaint's noble conduct rose above the prejudice against
Catholics and Black people that were prevalent in nineteenth-
century America.[11] He experienced racism daily on the
streets of New York. He had to walk to his clients' homes
because public omnibuses were for whites only. Once he and
Juliette even experienced discrimination from the Church
when they were refused entry to an event at today's Old Saint
Patrick's Cathedral, which his fundraising helped build. Historian Cyprian Davis notes: "His . . . strength of character
. . . enabled him not only to survive the racial prejudice of
his day . . . but to do so with grace and magnanimity. . . .
He remained throughout his life his own man because in
his fidelity he was God's."[12]

Sadly, Euphémie died in 1829 at age fourteen of tuberculosis. Toussaint's beloved Juliette, though twenty-two years
younger than he, died in 1851, and Toussaint died two years

[8] Ibid., 10, 21.

[9] Jones, *Pierre Toussaint*, 313.

[10] Cyprian Davis, O.S.B., *The History of Black Catholics in the United States*
(Chestnut Ridge, N.Y.: Crossroad, 1990), 94.

[11] Jones, *Pierre Toussaint*, 248.

[12] Davis, *History of Black Catholics*, 94.

later at the age of eighty-seven. Newspapers published glowing obituaries highlighting his faith and charity. His pastor, Father William Quinn, eulogized him by saying: "Though no relative was left to mourn him, yet many present would feel they had lost one who always had wise counsel for the rich, words of encouragement for the poor, and all would be grateful for having known him. . . . There were few left among the clergy superior in devotion and zeal for the Church and the glory of God, among laymen, none."[13]

Toussaint was originally buried in the cemetery at the Old Saint Patrick's Cathedral, but when his canonization cause was opened more than a century later, his body was exhumed and reinterred under the main altar in the present-day Saint Patrick's Cathedral. He is the only layman buried there. His canonization cause progressed further in 1996, when he was named Venerable in recognition of his heroic virtue.

[13] Lee, *Memoir of Pierre Toussaint*, 25.

MOTHER MARY ELIZABETH LANGE

Finding Freedom Serving God,
Sharing Freedom Serving Others

Servant of God Mother Mary Elizabeth Lange, O.S.P., found freedom in following God's will, which led her to co-found the first successful Roman Catholic religious order for Black women in the United States. Not only did the Oblate Sisters of Providence quietly prove that Black women could worthily wear a habit and live the consecrated life, but their mission to educate Black children freed youth from illiteracy and opened doors of opportunity to them.

Little is known about Elizabeth Clarissa Lange's early life. She is believed to have been born between 1784 to 1794 in Santiago de Cuba and reared in the French-speaking section of the city. Of African descent, she was well educated, spoke French, Spanish, and English, and likely came from a family of means. She described herself as "French to my soul".[1]

In the early 1800s, Elizabeth emigrated to the United States as a free woman of color, perhaps because of an 1808 government order for non-Spanish Cuban residents to vow loyalty to the Spanish king. By 1813 she was living in Baltimore, Maryland, which had a large population of

---

[1] Michael R. Heinlein, "Servant of God Mary Lange", in *Black Catholics on the Road to Sainthood*, ed. Michael R. Heinlein (Huntington, Ind.: Our Sunday Visitor, 2021), 67.

French-speaking Catholics, many of African descent, who had fled the Haitian Revolution.[2]

At the time, Maryland was a slave state and did not offer free public education to Black children, whether enslaved or free.[3] Seeing a need and using money from her family, Elizabeth and a friend, Black Haitian refugee Marie Magdaleine Balas, opened a free school for French-speaking children of color in her home. The women ran it for a decade before they could no longer afford to keep it open.

Providence intervened in 1827 when Sulpician Father James Hector Joubert, a French native and former government official in Haiti, became the catechist at Saint Mary's Seminary Chapel, which ministered to Baltimore's Haitian refugees. Aware that the Black Haitian children were struggling to learn their catechism because they could not read, he desired to open a school for them.[4] To ensure its stability, he also wanted to establish a religious order for women of color whose mission was to teach the children. Hearing about Elizabeth and Marie's school efforts, he reached out to them and discovered that in addition to sharing a desire to educate the children, the women felt a call to consecrated life, which they hadn't been able to answer because no orders were then open to Black women.

"Both of them told me that for more than ten years they had worked to consecrate themselves to God for this work, waiting patiently that in his own infinite goodness he would

Heinlein, *Mary Lange*, 67–68.

[3] Lauren Morton, "Mary Elizabeth Clovis Lange (c. 1784–1882)", Archives of Maryland (Biographical Series), Maryland State Archives, August 24, 2005, msa.maryland.gov/megafile/msa/speccol/sc3500/sc3520/013500/013580/html/13580bio.html.

[4] Davis, *History of Black Catholics*, 99.

show them the way", Father Joubert wrote in his diary. "Assured of their good will I felt bound to prepare the way."[5]

When he secured permission to establish the religious congregation from his superior, Archbishop James Whitfield, Father Joubert recorded the prelate's positive response: "It is not lightly but with reflection that I approved your project. I knew and saw the finger of God; let us not oppose his holy will."[6]

On June 13, 1828, Elizabeth, Marie, and Haitian refugee Rosine Boegue, opened the first Black Catholic school in the United States—thirty-five years before one of the great documents of human freedom, the Emancipation Proclamation, was written.[7] Originally called the Oblate School for Colored Girls, it continues today as Saint Frances Academy, a coeducational high school named after the Oblate Sisters' first convent.

On July 2, 1829, another historic event took place when Elizabeth, Marie, and Rosine were joined by Baltimore-born Almeide Duchemin Maxis in professing vows as the first Oblate Sisters of Providence.[8] The women consecrated themselves to God and to the Christian education of children of color.[9] Elizabeth took the religious name Mary

[5] M. Reginald Gerdes, "To Educate and Evangelize: Black Catholic Schools of the Oblate Sisters of Providence (1828–1880)", *U.S. Catholic Historian* 7, nos. 2/3: 187.

[6] Davis, *History of Black Catholics*, 100.

[7] "Our History", *Saint Frances Academy*, accessed November 8, 2023, sfacademy.org/about-us/.

[8] Davis, *History of Black Catholics*, 100. Almeide Duchemin Maxis later went on to cofound the Servants of the Immaculate Heart of Mary in Michigan, which is not a Black order. She is the first U.S.-born religious sister of African descent.

[9] Catholic News Agency, "Sainthood Cause Advances for Mother Mary Lange, Educator Who Fought Racism", *National Catholic Register*, December

and became the first superior general of the congregation. Mother Mary Elizabeth served three terms as superior general, three terms as mistress of novices, and a term as assistant general.

The Rule of community life the Oblate Sisters followed was written by Father Joubert, but according to historian Thaddeus Posey, Mother Mary Elizabeth Lange "gave that Rule life—she was the spirit of the Rule . . . her zeal for the children and her tireless efforts for the community set an example for all the sisters."[10]

As a devout, educated free woman, Mother Mary Elizabeth knew that a Christian education would free not only her students' minds, but their spirits as well. Posey writes: "Mother Mary Lange was an educator with a vision of the black community as to what could be realized and an inspiration from God as to how it might be accomplished." She taught "those who were considered unteachable" and nurtured in them "the self-confidence to become productive citizens".[11]

Mother Mary Elizabeth and her nuns were pioneers "in a hostile environment that did not want 'religious women of color'". In fact, to some, "the very notion of 'religious women of color' was a contradiction in terms."[12] The Oblate Sisters were evicted from their first rental after just six months when the landlord learned they were run-

---

11, 2019, ncregister.com/news/sainthood-cause-advances-for-mother-mary -lange-educator-who-fought-racism.

[10] Thaddeus J. Posey, O.F.M. Cap., "Praying in the Shadows: The Oblate Sisters of Providence, a Look at Nineteenth-Century Black Catholic Spirituality", *U.S. Catholic Historian* 12, no. 1 (Winter 1994): 18, 24.

[11] Ibid., 19.

[12] Ibid., 25.

ning a school for Black children. They encountered more discrimination as they searched for another site until they finally secured a new location a month later with the help of a white Haitian refugee.

"In their diaries", reported the *Baltimore Magazine*, "the sisters worried about the possibility of being lynched for teaching colored children, or just for being a black woman with the audacity to wear a nun's habit."[13] However, throughout their trials and persecutions, Mother Mary Elizabeth transmitted her courage, faith, and perseverance to her sisters, saying, "Our sole wish is to do the will of God."

In 1832 a cholera epidemic hit Baltimore, and the Oblate Sisters were asked if four of them could help nurse the sick poor, as the Sisters of Charity had sent just four volunteers after being asked for eight. The city official made the request through Father Joubert, who said he would ask the Oblates but cautioned that while "the Sisters of Charity were by the spirit of their institute obliged to look after the sick", the Oblates' vocation was the education of Black children. When he asked, though, all eleven of the Oblate Sisters volunteered. Of them, four were sent, including Mother Mary Elizabeth.[14]

In 1835, the Oblate Sisters were asked by the Sulpician superior if two of them could do housekeeping at Saint Mary's Seminary. Mother Mary Elizabeth responded affirmatively and graciously while setting boundaries to protect the sisters' status as free, consecrated women of color. To protect the partial cloister their Rule required, she requested that the

---

[13] Dean Storm, "Waiting for a Miracle", *Baltimore Magazine*, June 1997, msa.maryland.gov/megafile/msa/speccol/sc3500/sc3520/013500/013580/pdf/baltjune1997.pdf.
[14] Davis, *History of Black Catholics*, 101.

sisters not "have any relation with the other servants and
outside people than our obligations require". The Sulpician
superior, Father Louis Deluol, responded with "unaccus-
tomed equality", saying, "You write the paper which shall
contain the conditions under which you will come and I
shall sign it."[15] Later, after one of the original sisters sent
to do domestic work died, Mother Mary Elizabeth took her
place.

"What were the works of Mother Lange?" mused former archivist Oblates Sister Reginald Gerdes. "We know
of her private school in the early 1800s, of her academy in
1828 and of her religious foundation in 1829. But, there was
also an orphanage, a widow's home, spiritual direction, religious education classes and vocational training. The early
sisters did home visiting and conducted night schools so
black adults could learn to read and write. When the Civil
War was over, Baltimore was flooded with black war orphans. Mother Mary gathered 60 of them and began a new
era of caring for destitute children. She was a religious pioneer."[16]

After a life of service, Mother Mary Elizabeth died in
her room at the Oblate Sisters' Saint Frances Convent on
February 3, 1882. Nearly two hundred years after the founding of the Oblate Sisters of Providence, her order continues, as does the first school she established, today's Saint

[15] Diane Batts Morrow, "Outsiders Within: The Oblate Sisters of Providence in the 1830s Church and Society", U.S. Catholic Historian 15, no. 2
(Spring 1997): 51–52.
[16] Sr. Reginald Gerdes, "By Her Works", in What We Have Seen and
Heard: Essays and Stories from Black Catholics of Baltimore, ed. Archdiocese
of Baltimore (Baltimore: Cathedral Foundation Press, 2005), quoted in
"Mother Mary Lange", Mother Mary Lange Guild, accessed November 8,
2023, motherlange.org/mother-lange.

Frances Academy. In starting the order, Mother Mary Elizabeth demonstrated "the virtue of black women in defi-
ance of prevailing social attitudes".[17] She and her sisters
transcended racism, injustice, and suffering by serving the
oppressed. In doing so, they brought hope and faith to
the Black community and empowered countless youth and
adults with education. Saint Frances Academy remains a beacon of hope for inner-city Baltimore youth. Mother Mary
Elizabeth's cause for canonization was opened in 1991, and
she was named Servant of God in that first step of the process.

---

[17] Morrow, "Outsiders", 53.

CARDINAL PATRICK O'BOYLE

Desegregation and Civil Rights Pioneer

In 1948 Archbishop Patrick O'Boyle became the first resident archbishop of the then-new Archdiocese of Washington, D.C. The legacy of his twenty-five years in that role and of his sixty-six-year priesthood overall is that of a champion of social justice and civil rights.[1] In recognition of his work to ensure equality and freedom for all, he was made a cardinal in 1967.

In 1949, five years before the U.S. Supreme Court outlawed school segregation, Archbishop O'Boyle desegregated the Catholic schools and churches of the capital city, which was still under Jim Crow rule.[2] To avoid turmoil, he acted prudently and purposefully. He met the strongest resistance in the counties of southern Maryland that belonged to his diocese.[3] There, in August 1956, Archbishop O'Boyle spent a day with representatives of the major parishes of Saint Mary's County, who implored the archbishop to delay

[1] "Former Archbishops of Washington: Patrick A. O'Boyle", *Archdiocese of Washington*, accessed November 8, 2023, adw.org/about-us/who-we-are/former-archbishops/.

[2] Bart Barnes, "Cardinal O'Boyle Dies at 91", *The Washington Post*, August 11, 1987, washingtonpost.com/archive/politics/1987/08/11/cardinal-oboyle-dies-at-91/d8f814ef-ed6b-42e4-b5c9-d7d9c929f440/.

[3] "Statement by Archbishop Patrick A. Cardinal O'Boyle", *American Catholic History Classroom*, accessed November 8, 2023, cuomeka.wrlc.org/exhibits/show/the-catholic-church--bishops--/documents/statement-by-archbishop-patric.

integrating the schools until the state mandated integration for public schools. Some claimed integration would not be possible for a decade. "Well, gentlemen," responded the prelate, "we're going to do it tomorrow."[4]

Gradually, integration was achieved without major incident. It is said that both before and after the 1954 Supreme Court decision banning school segregation, Chief Justice Earl Warren conferred with Archbishop O'Boyle to learn how the Catholic entities had been desegregated.[5]

Patrick Aloysius O'Boyle was born on July 18, 1896 to Irish immigrants Michael and Mary (Muldoon) O'Boyle in Scranton, Pennsylvania. When Patrick was ten-and-a-half years old, his steelworker father died. Patrick continued to attend his parish school but took on a second paper route to help support his mother and extended family. In 1910, at age fourteen, he temporarily dropped out of school to work full time as a messenger but the next year returned, and he graduated from Saint Thomas Preparatory High School in 1912. After graduating from Saint Thomas College (now the University of Scranton) in 1916, he attended Saint Joseph Seminary in Yonkers, New York and was ordained a priest in 1921.[6]

Father O'Boyle's first assignment was at New York's Saint Columba's Parish. Five years later, he was named director of the Catholic Charities organization that helped care for orphans and foster children. During this time, he entered a graduate program at the New York School of Social Work from which he graduated in 1932. The next year, he helped

[4] Morris J. MacGregor, *Steadfast in the Faith: The Life of Patrick Cardinal O'Boyle* (Washington, D.C.: The Catholic University of America Press, 2006), 194–95.

[5] Barnes, "Cardinal O'Boyle". See also MacGregor, *Steadfast*, 187.

[6] MacGregor, *Steadfast*, 1, 15–20, 31.

found a social work program at the Catholic University of America. Later assignments included directing a home for homeless children on Staten Island, then directing Catholic War Relief Services for overseas soldiers, POWs, and refugees during World War II. In 1947 he was named director of Catholic Charities in New York. Three months later, he was named archbishop of Washington by Pope Pius XII.[7]

Archbishop O'Boyle's working-class upbringing and his early ministry in charitable and social work planted the seeds for the social justice and civil rights advocacy that marked his episcopal ministry. Convinced that racism is incompatible with Christianity, he was an ardent supporter of racial justice and equality. He gave the invocation at the 1963 March on Washington for Jobs and Freedom where the Reverend Martin Luther King Jr. delivered his stirring "I Have a Dream" speech. "Send in our midst the Holy Spirit to open the eyes of all to the great truth that all men are equal in Your sight", Archbishop O'Boyle prayed. "Let us understand that simple justice demands that the rights of all be honored by every man."[8]

In April 1964, Archbishop O'Boyle chaired the Interreligious Convocation on Civil Rights. The event for religious leaders aimed to show support for the Civil Rights bill, which was being debated by Congress. In his opening remarks, Archbishop O'Boyle called passage of the law "a

[7] "Biography of Patrick Aloysius Cardinal O'Boyle", *Patrick Cardinal O'Boyle Council, Knights of Columbus*, accessed November 8, 2023, oboyle.dc knights.org/index.php/about-us/about-cardinal-o-boyle.

[8] Patrick A. O'Boyle, "Invocation by Archbishop Patrick O'Boyle for 1963 March on Washington", August 28, 1963, Lincoln Memorial, Washington, D.C., Archdiocese of Washington, adw.org/invocation-by-archbishop -patrick-oboyle-for-1963-march-on-washington/.

moral obligation".[9] The Civil Rights Act, which ended discrimination based on race, color, religion, sex, or national origin, was passed and signed into law in July 1964. It ended Jim Crow laws and is considered the nation's benchmark civil rights legislation.

Three years later, when Archbishop O'Boyle was elevated to cardinal, he humbly stated: "In a very real sense this honor which has come to me is an expression of the Holy Father's gratitude, not only to the priests, religious and devoted laity of the Washington Archdiocese, but also to the many clergy and laymen of other faiths who have labored beside us in attacking the problem of racial and social injustice, which are our common concern."[10]

In 1972, Cesar Chavez, leader of the United Farmworkers movement, called for a boycott of lettuce to support harvesters' efforts to unionize to gain fair wages and humane working conditions. Long a supporter of unionism, Cardinal O'Boyle, in a Labor Day statement for his diocese, urged the public's support for the farmworkers' effort. He likened the immigrant laborers' deplorable situation to that of his Scranton relatives and neighbors from his childhood. The AFL-CIO noticed and praised his social justice leadership.[11]

Not only was he at the forefront of those who spoke out against the evil of racism and worked for equal opportunity for all in employment, education, and housing, but his passion for civil rights extended to religious freedom as well.

[9] "Archbishop Patrick Cardinal O'Boyle Prayer on Civil Rights Act", *American Catholic History Classroom*, accessed November 8, 2023, cuomeka .wrlc.org/exhibits/show/the-catholic-church--bishops--/documents/archbish op-patrick-cardinal-o-.

[10] Stephanie Jacobe, "The First Cardinal Archbishop of Washington", *Archdiocese of Washington*, accessed November 8, 2023, adw.org/the-first-cardinal -archbishop-of-washington/.

[11] MacGregor, *Steadfast*, 393.

During the Second Vatican Council, he was involved in the Declaration on Religious Liberty, which asserts that the human person has a legal right to religious freedom.[12]

In his biography of Cardinal O'Boyle, *Steadfast in the Faith*, Morris MacGregor notes that the prelate was "honestly amazed that the son of a poor steelworker had become a cardinal".[13] Cardinal O'Boyle retired at age seventy-seven in 1973. He died at age ninety-one on August 10, 1987. In a statement acknowledging the cardinal's death, then-President Ronald Reagan recalled the prelate's fight for freedom for all. "Cardinal O'Boyle never ceased to champion the rights and the dignity of all human life, and he never hesitated to take action in its defense", President Reagan said. "The life of Cardinal Patrick O'Boyle paralleled the course of this century and epitomized the finest qualities of a turbulent era in the life of America and in the world."[14]

---

[12] Ibid., 269–71.
[13] Ibid., 403.
[14] Ronald Reagan, "Statement on the Death of Patrick Cardinal O'Boyle" (August 11, 1987), *Ronald Reagan Presidential Library & Museum*, reaganlibrary .gov/archives/speech/statement-death-patrick-cardinal-oboyle.

II

PERSEVERANCE

DEFINING PERSEVERANCE

No one who believes in Jesus Christ can avoid the call to do "good works." According to Saint Paul, God created us precisely for this purpose (Eph 2:10). Jesus himself teaches that only "he who *does* the will of my Father" will "enter the kingdom of heaven" (Mt 7:21, emphasis added). *Doing* is necessary. And this divine will engages not only the soul—prayer, faith, purity, forgiveness—but the body: our hands and feet. God summons his people to action. In Matthew 25:31–46, the "righteous" are those who feed the hungry, give drink to the thirsty, welcome the stranger, clothe the naked, and visit the prisoner. The Good Samaritan, in Christ's parable, does not just pity the man on the street but tends his wounds and pays his bills (Lk 10:30–37). Mary of Bethany pours a whole container of expensive oil on the Lord's feet to anoint him, much to the dismay of Judas (Jn 12:1–8). For those who believe, God's will—when it is clear—is worth living out whatever the cost.

Sometimes, doing the good seems not just costly, but close to impossible. Servant of God Father Augustus Tolton, whose powerful homilies attracted Catholics of all races, was maligned by fellow priests in nineteenth-century New Jersey merely because he was Black. Servant of God Mother Henriette Delille, who, after losing her children as a young single mother, experienced a profound conversion, was repeatedly turned away by orders in Louisiana for her Creole heritage. When college student Diane Nash began organizing nonviolent protests against segregation on interstate buses in the early 1960s, President John F. Kennedy himself asked her to stop. Yet all three of these Catholics took seriously the Letter to the Hebrews: "You have need of *endurance*"—in Greek, *hypomonē*, meaning also *perseverance*—"so that you may do the will of God" (Heb 10:36, emphasis added).[1]

Just as the four men in Mark's Gospel, finding no path through the crowds to reach Jesus, lower their paralytic friend down to the Lord from the roof in order to be healed (Mk 2:3–11), so any Christian determined to obey God can, in faith, find imaginative ways forward, even if the road is not the one he had first expected. As Pope Francis once remarked, "Sometimes we allow discouragement to overcome us. . . . Instead, Jesus says we can also be *clever* in following the Gospel, *awake* and *attentive* to discern reality, and *creative* to find good solutions for us and others."[2] So it was with Father Tolton, Mother Delille, and Diane Nash, all of whom discovered unexpected trails ahead and found themselves doing more than they had dreamed. This is the nature of that "perseverance and energy" which Pope Pius X extolled in 1906, when French Catholics, oppressed by anticlerical laws, took a stand for religious freedom in their country—"not by violence, but by firmness."[3] Such lively, energetic, creative perseverance is at the heart of true heroism.

---

[1] See Benedict XVI, encyclical letter *Spe Salvi* (November 30, 2007), no. 9.

[2] Francis, Angelus (September 18, 2022).

[3] Pius X, encyclical letter *Gravissimo officii munere* (August 10, 1906), no. 11.

CHURCH DOCUMENTS
ON PERSEVERANCE

from U.S. Bishops, *Brothers and Sisters to Us: Pastoral Letter on Racism* (1979)

This is the mystery of our Church, that all men and women are brothers and sisters, all one in Christ, all bear the image of the Eternal God. The Church is truly universal, embracing all races, for it is "the visible sacrament of this saving unity." . . .

The prophetic voice of the Church, which is to be heard in every generation and even to the ends of the earth, must not be muted—especially not by the counter witness of some of its own people. . . .

There must be no turning back along the road of justice, no sighing for bygone times of privilege, no nostalgia for simple solutions from another age. For we are children of the age to come, when the first shall be last and the last shall be first, when blessed are they who serve Christ the Lord in all His brothers and sisters, especially those who are poor and suffer injustice.[1]

---

[1] National Conference of Catholic Bishops, *Brothers and Sisters to Us: U.S. Bishops' Pastoral Letter on Racism in Our Day* (Washington, D.C.: United States Catholic Conference, 1979).

from Archbishop Joseph Kurtz, "Statement on the Fiftieth Anniversary of the Civil Rights Act" (2014)

We honor the many civic, business, and religious leaders, students, laborers, educators and all others of good will who courageously stood up for racial justice against bigotry, violence, ignorance, and fear. We remember with deep gratitude the countless personal sacrifices they made, sacrifices that all too often included hardship, violence, and even death. We honor the victory they won after such a long and sustained civil and legislative struggle. . . .

The Gospel requires ongoing personal and social transformation. Respecting the dignity of each person is paramount as we seek to spread the beauty of God's truth throughout our world. We cannot give in to discouragement. As Pope Francis reminds us, "Bringing the Gospel is bringing God's power to pluck up and break down evil and violence, to destroy and overthrow the barriers of selfishness, intolerance and hatred, so as to build a new world."[2]

[2] Archbishop Joseph Kurtz, President, United States Conference of Catholic Bishops, "Statement on the Occasion of the 50th Anniversary of the Civil Rights Act", USCCB press release, September 9, 2014, usccb.org/issues-and -action/cultural-diversity/african-american/upload/2014-09-Kurtz-Statement -on-Racism.pdf.

4

MOTHER HENRIETTE DELILLE

Humble Servant of Slaves

The life of Venerable Henriette Delille, a French-speaking Creole, is one of steadfast perseverance against racism. She overcame family resistance and pre–Civil War discrimination in society and in the Church to pursue consecrated life and founded the second religious order in the United States for Black women. After her life dedicated to serving free and enslaved people of color, when Henriette died, her obituary declared: "For the love of Jesus Christ, she made herself the humble servant of slaves."[1]

Henriette was born in 1812 in New Orleans, Louisiana, to a free Creole mother of Spanish, French, and African heritage and a white French father. She was the youngest of three children born to Marie-Josephe Pouponne Dias and Jean-Baptiste Delille-Sarpy. The couple had a common-law union as interracial marriage was prohibited.[2]

Henriette was reared to eventually enter such a relationship, known as *placage*, in which a wealthy white man cohabited with a woman of color. The arrangement could provide a comfortable, albeit illegitimate, life to the women

[1] *Henriette Delille Official Site*, accessed November 8, 2023, henriettedelille .com.

[2] Kim Chatelain, "The First Real New Orleans Saint? Henriette Delille's Path to Canonization", *Nola.com*, March 2, 2017, nola.com/archive/article_fd b34525-b68d-5910-9bfe-931c3acc275d.html.

and children but was precarious, as the men often also had legitimate families.

As a teen, Henriette may have had a *placage* union.[3] Church records indicate she buried two sons who, sadly, died before the age of three.[4] Baptized Catholic as a child, Henriette was confirmed in 1834 at age twenty-two. Biographer Michael Heinlein notes, "The sacrament of confirmation . . . was received in those days by only the most devout in practice of the faith."[5]

Henriette had experienced a profound conversion and had turned away from the *placage* system her family encouraged her to enter, seeing it as contrary to the sanctity of marriage. She felt called to religious life but was denied entry into the local Catholic orders because of her African heritage.[6]

Resolute despite rejection, in 1836 Henriette penned her testimony of faith in a prayer book: "I believe in God. I hope in God. I love. I wish to live and die for God." That year, on the feast of Mary's Presentation, she wrote a rule of life for an order called Sisters of the Presentation of the Blessed Virgin Mary, which later became the Sisters of the Holy Family. The members lived at home and were called "sister", although the group was not an official order. Their mission was to care for the sick, to aid the poor, and to

[3] "Healed Aneurysm Investigated as Possible Miracle for Creole Nun's Beatification", *Catholic News Agency*, August 30, 2019, catholicnewsagency.com/news/42139/healed-aneurysm-investigated-as-possible-miracle-for-creole-nuns-beatification.

[4] "Quick Facts".

[5] Michael Heinlein, "Venerable Henriette Delille", in *Black Catholics on the Road to Sainthood*, ed. Michael R. Heinlein (Huntington, Ind.: Our Sunday Visitor, 2021), 41.

[6] Josh Johnson, "Delille: A School of Perseverance and Patience", in *Black Catholics on the Road to Sainthood*, ed. Michael R. Heinlein (Huntington, Ind.: Our Sunday Visitor, 2021), 46–47.

instruct the ignorant.[7] Their instruction included both academic and religious education.

They also made a three-part pledge: first, to be pious women above reproach—especially important because women of color were seen as licentious because of the *placage* custom;[8] second, to help each other spiritually and materially in their ministry; third, to serve their people.[9]

Serving enslaved and free people of color alongside Henriette were longtime friends and order cofounders Juliette Gaudin and Josephine Charles, who had also rejected the *placage* lifestyle.[10] Their catechetical efforts were extraordinary: in the 1830s their names appear regularly as baptism and confirmation sponsors and as witnesses to marriages. They discouraged *placage* unions and urged slave couples to have their common-law relationships blessed. Their educational work was especially courageous, as teaching the enslaved was illegal and could be punished with imprisonment or death.[11]

---

[7] Edward T. Brett, "Race Issues and Conflict in Nineteenth- and Early Twentieth-Century Religious Life: The New Orleans Sisters of the Holy Family", *U.S. Catholic Historian* 29, no. 1 (Winter 2011): 114–15.

[8] Brett, "Race Issues", 118.

[9] Virginia Meacham Gould and Charles E. Nolan, "Introduction", in Mary Bernard Deggs, *No Cross, No Crown: Black Nuns in Nineteenth Century New Orleans*, ed. Virginia Meacham Gould and Charles E. Nolan (Bloomington, Ind.: Indiana University Press, 2001) xxxi–xxxiii.

[10] Johnson, "Delille", 41; Brett, "Race Issues", 114. See also CNA/EWTN News, "This 18th Century Creole Nun Risked Her Life to Teach Slaves", *The Catholic Register*, February 20, 2017, catholicregister.org/home/internatio nal/item/24380-this-18th-century-creole-nun-risked-her-life-to-teach-slaves.

[11] CNA/EWTN News, "Creole Nun"; Gould and Nolan, "Introduction", xxxii; "Dates and Events in the Life of Venerable Henriette Delille", Henri etteDelille.com, accessed November 8, 2023, henriettedelille.com/henriette -delille.

On November 21, 1842, the order, under the name Sisters of the Holy Family, was established with the approval and support of Bishop Antoine Blanc and his vicar general, Father Étienne Rousselon. Now Henriette and Juliette moved into a home on Saint Bernard Street in the French Quarter as a convent where they could live in community. Josephine joined them a few months later.[12]

The convent also served as a home for elderly Black people the sisters cared for: the Hospice of the Holy Family was the nation's first Catholic home for the aged and continues today as Lafon Nursing Facility of the Holy Family.[13] During New Orleans' yellow fever epidemics in 1853 and 1897, the sisters also used the home to nurse the sick.[14]

In 1850, Henriette used a loan and money she had inherited from her mother to buy a larger house for the convent, also in the French Quarter, on Bayou Road. This enabled the congregation to add members and to expand their ministry.[15] On October 15, 1852, the three cofounders made their first canonical vows as religious and Henriette was named mother superior.[16] Historian Cyprian Davis notes: "Under civil law, however, they were not recognized as religious. In fact, it would seem that the civil authorities in this city of slavery tolerated the existence of the sisters because of the work they did in nursing the sick poor among the black population. The sisters . . . [also] established an orphanage . . . and in addition continued to operate a school for girls, established in 1850, and to teach the children catechism in

[12] Theresa A. Rector, "Black Nuns as Educators", *The Journal of Negro Education* 51, no. 3 (Summer 1982): 246.

[13] Rector, "Black Nuns", 246.

[14] CNA/EWTN News, "Creole Nun".

[15] Brett, "Race Issues", 116.

[16] Gould and Nolan, *No Cross, No Crown*, 3.

two New Orleans parishes."[17] As the years passed, the sisters' ministry spread throughout Louisiana and beyond.

Because the laws and social mores of the times, which included anti-Catholic misconceptions and prejudice, did not permit public recognition of the Black congregation, Father Rousselon and now-Archbishop Blanc kept the creation of the order low key.[18] The sisters made their vows in private and they were not allowed to wear a habit, the outward sign of their being consecrated women and mark of their specific order.[19]

When their community was established in 1842, the sisters wore blue percale dresses with black bonnets. After professing their vows, they wore black dresses. It wasn't until "after the Civil War had ended (1865) and legal restrictions against African Americans were mitigated" that the local bishop granted permission to the sisters to wear a habit. Unfortunately, in 1866 the process to acquire a habit unique to the order was interrupted, and they didn't receive one until 1872.[20]

Principal foundress Mother Henriette never wore a habit, as she died ten years before the order received one. In the 1960s, when many religious sisters gave up wearing habits after Vatican II, the Holy Family Sisters kept theirs. They see their habit as a privilege they suffered long to get.[21]

Mother Henriette died of exhaustion and pleurisy at age fifty on November 17, 1862, just months after Union troops

[17] Cyprian Davis, O.S.B., *The History of Black Catholics in the United States* (Chestnut Ridge, N.Y.: Crossroad, 1990), 107.

[18] Brett, "Race Issues", 118.

[19] Tracey Fessenden, "The Sisters of the Holy Family and the Veil of Race", *Religion and American Culture: A Journal of Interpretation* 10, no. 2 (Summer 2000): 188.

[20] Brett, "Race Issues", 121–22.

[21] Fessenden, "Sisters of the Holy Family", 188.

seized New Orleans during the Civil War.[22] Historian Edward T. Brett notes that throughout her quest to establish a religious order, the "negative effects of racial prejudice permeated" her efforts. "It was the underlying factor that caused (the sisters) to suffer countless humiliations and indignities at the hands of church officials and secular society." Throughout it all, Mother Henriette led and persevered with Christian charity. Her order endures today. Mother Henriette's cause for canonization was opened in 1988. She was declared Venerable in 2010 by Pope Benedict XVI in recognition of her life of heroic virtue.

---

[22] Davis, *History of Black Catholics*, 107.

FATHER AUGUSTUS TOLTON

First Black Catholic Priest in the United States

"Now you are free. Never, never forget the goodness of the Lord." Those were the words spoken by Augustus Tolton's mother in 1862 after safely falling to her knees in the free state of Illinois, following a harrowing flight from slavery in Missouri with her two little sons and baby daughter. They had run miles at night, then crossed the wide Mississippi River in a broken-down rowboat while being shot at by Confederate pursuers.[1]

He was only eight at the time, but Augustus never did forget. Through perseverance and faith in the God who had saved him from both slavery to sin and slavery at the hands of men, Augustus grew up to become the first Catholic priest in the United States publicly known to be Black. (Three brothers of Irish and African American ancestry— James, Patrick, and Sherwood Healy—had previously been ordained priests, but they were never identified as Black.[2])

Augustus was born in Brush Creek, Missouri, on April 1, 1854, to Martha Jane (Chisley) and Peter Paul Tolton, who were Catholic. His parents had him baptized at Saint Peter Church on May 29. His baptismal certificate indicates

[1] Caroline Hemesath, *From Slave to Priest: The Inspirational Story of Father Augustine Tolton (1854–1897)* (San Francisco: Ignatius Press, 2006), 32.
[2] Ibid., 18.

his slave status, stating, "Property of Stephen Eliot",[3] the plantation owner on whose land the family lived. His wife served as Augustus' sponsor. At the time, slaves were often baptized into the faith of their "owners".[4]

When the Civil War broke out in 1861, Augustus' father escaped to Saint Louis and joined the Union Army to fight against slavery. Unbeknownst to his family, he died of dysentery shortly thereafter.[5] Martha Jane was fearful after a year without word from her husband, but faith in God's goodness (ultimately shown in help along their journey) drove her courageous exodus with her children.[6] Once they went ashore in Illinois, they made their way twenty-one miles to Quincy, which was home to many refugee slaves.

In Quincy, Martha Jane found work in a tobacco factory. When Augustus was nine and his brother Charley was ten, they too began working at the factory—ten hours a day, six days a week. Sadly, that winter Charley caught pneumonia and died.[7] It was 1863, the year President Abraham Lincoln's Emancipation Proclamation legally freed all slaves in the Confederacy.[8] Later in life, Augustus would recall his mother's story about his father's last words over his sleeping children before leaving to fight for freedom: "They must

[3] Ibid., 28.

[4] Harold Burke-Sivers, *Father Augustus Tolton: The Slave Who Became the First African American Priest* (Birmingham, Ala.: EWTN Publishing, 2018), 9.

[5] Joseph Perry, "Father Augustus Tolton, 1854–1897", *Archdiocese of Chicago*, accessed November 8, 2023, tolton.archchicago.org/documents/160456 1/1604725/Tolton+Biography+-+PDF/d8d2f8ac-b0c6-4180-b474-0ea68b484 9ba.

[6] Hemesath, *From Slave to Priest*, 30–31.

[7] Hemesath, *From Slave to Priest*, 39.

[8] "Fr. Tolton's Life and Times", *Archdiocese of Chicago*, accessed November 8, 2023, tolton.archchicago.org/about/life-and-times.

not be slaves; they must learn to read and write; they must have a better life than we had."[9]

In 1865, at the end of the Civil War, Martha Jane learned of her husband's death when his name appeared on the Union Army's casualty list. He was among the 63,178 Black soldiers who died for the northern army.[10] That year, Martha Jane enrolled eleven-year-old Augustus in the parish school of Saint Boniface Church, where the family worshiped, so he could attend during the three months of the year the tobacco factory was closed. While the pastor of the largely German congregation, Father Herman Schaeffermeyer, and the nuns staffing the school were welcoming, the parishioners were not. Augustus was withdrawn within a month due to his being bullied and to threats against the administrators.[11]

Three years later, Augustus' transferred to a public school, but his two-month experience there was also unhappy. There, he experienced discrimination from mixed-race students and was teased because he could not read at age fourteen. When the pastor of the family's new parish, Saint Peter's (initially named Saint Lawrence's), learned Augustus was attending public school, he promised to make it possible for the teen to attend their parish school—again, during the months the tobacco factory was closed.[12]

Father Peter McGirr, a native Irishman, was true to his word and became a lifelong friend to Augustus. The School Sisters of Notre Dame who staffed the school, particularly Sister Herlinde Sick, tutored Augustus to help him catch up.

[9] Hemesath, *From Slave to Priest*, 36.

[10] Perry, "Father Augustus Tolton", 6.

[11] Ibid., 6–7.

[12] Ibid., 7–8.

They also trained him as an altar server. Augustus attended Saint Peter School three months a year until he graduated in 1872 at age eighteen. He often fondly recalled: "As long as I was in that school, I was safe. Everyone was kind to me. I learned the alphabet, spelling, reading and arithmetic."[13]

Augustus' love for the Mass showed in his daily attendance at Saint Peter's as an altar server before starting his shift at the tobacco factory. Both Father McGirr and Father Schaeffermeyer believed he had a vocation to the priesthood. This affirmed the call Augustus felt in his heart, a call that had begun when he learned that Christ's command at the Last Supper to "Do this in commemoration of me" referred to the celebration of the Mass.[14]

After Augustus graduated from Saint Peter School, his former pastors provided for tutoring to prepare him for seminary. In 1878 he was accepted at Saint Francis College (now Quincy University) as a special advanced student. In 1880, after years of rejection by American seminaries who refused to accept a Black student, Augustus started at the Pontifical Urban College for the Propagation of the Faith in Rome, which still trains missionary priests. He was twenty-five and desired to be a missionary in Africa. Accepted as an equal at the seminary where he was called "Gus from the U.S.", he described his time there as one of "receiving a full measure of earthly happiness".[15]

He was thirty-two when he was ordained a priest on Holy Saturday, April 24, 1886, at Saint John Lateran Church in Rome. The previous day, Good Friday, he had received startling news: instead of going to Africa, he was to be sent to the United States—to Quincy. Cardinal Simeoni,

[13] Ibid., 7–8.
[14] Hemesath, *From Slave to Priest*, 53.
[15] Ibid., 135.

the prefect, had ultimately vetoed the plan to send Augustus to Africa, saying: "America needs black priests. America has been called the most enlightened nation. We will
see whether it deserves that honor. If the United States has
never seen a black priest, it must see one now."[16]

Father Augustus celebrated his first Mass in Rome's Saint
Peter's Basilica on April 25, Easter Sunday. At the request
of nun friends, the first Mass he celebrated in the United
States was on July 7 in Saint Mary's Hospital chapel of Hobo-
ken, New Jersey. On July 18, he celebrated his first Mass
in Quincy at Saint Boniface Church, his boyhood parish.
There, as he thanked those who helped him become a priest,
Father Augustus said emphatically, "Above all, I want to
thank my mother."[17] After the Mass, he also gave his priestly
blessing to her before granting it to the hundreds of others
who sought it.[18]

He started his priestly ministry in Quincy as pastor of the
primarily Black congregation of Saint Joseph Church. The
assignment seemed providential as the parish grew out of
a school for Black children he had helped found as a layman years earlier.[19] Known for his pastoral zeal, inspiring
preaching, and beautiful singing voice, the tall Black pastor
drew white Catholics from neighboring churches as well.
This resulted in jealousy and outright discrimination from
other pastors, who bemoaned the loss of parishioners and
their financial support. The situation reached a climax when
the bishop supported the local dean who told Father Gus to
minister to Black parishioners only.[20]

[16] Ibid., 154.
[17] Ibid., 166.
[18] Perry, "Father Augustus Tolton", 19.
[19] Hemesath, *From Slave to Priest*, 102.
[20] Ibid., 187.

While some in Quincy were trying to get rid of him, others elsewhere wanted to have him for their own. A Black charitable group called the Saint Augustine Society wanted Father Gus to help them establish a congregation in Chicago.[21] In 1889 he received permission to leave Quincy to minister in Chicago, where he served as pastor of a mission to Black Catholics that met in a church basement and was put in charge of all Black ministry in the diocese.

Under the direction of "good Father Gus", as he was affectionately called, within two years the mission congregation grew and moved to a storefront they named Saint Monica's Chapel. The pastor and his flock's desire for a permanent church was realized in 1894 when stately Saint Monica Church was dedicated. The new church, which was complete enough for use with plans for a future addition, was made possible with donations, including from heiress and religious order foundress Saint Katharine Drexel.

Father Gus had grown his ministry from thirty people who gathered in the church basement to some six hundred Black Catholics across Chicago. Although by now a popular national speaker, he aimed to put his impoverished congregation first. For years, parishioners had noticed he carried on despite bouts of weakness and ill health.[22]

In an 1890 letter to a priest, Father Gus described his vast mission as the sole Black priest in the nation: "I wish at this moment that there were 27 Father Toltons or colored priests at any rate who could supply the demands", he wrote,

[21] *Encyclopaedia Britannica Online*, s.v. "Augustus Tolton", by Matt Stefon, updated July 5, 2023, britannica.com/biography/Augustus-Tolton.
[22] Hemesath, *From Slave to Priest*, 209.

referring to the number of invitations he had to preach and advise. Historian Cyprian Davis writes: "His reputation . . . had spread far beyond Chicago. In a sense, he was the priest for all African Americans."[23]

Indeed, when the First Black Catholic Congress was held in Washington, D.C., in 1889, Father Augustus was the main speaker.[24] Recalling his humble beginnings as a child slave, he credited the Church with educating him and nurturing his faith and his priestly vocation. "The Catholic Church deplores a double slavery—that of the mind and that of the body", he said. "She endeavors to free us of both."[25] Through the Church, beginning with his baptism, God had freed Father Gus—spirit, mind, and body. He called the Church "a true liberator of the race".[26]

Father Gus died suddenly on July 9, 1897, after falling unconscious with sunstroke during a Chicago heat wave. He was forty-three. In keeping with his wishes, he was buried in Quincy in the cemetery of Saint Peter's Church, where he had received First Communion and Confirmation. The monument marking his grave memorializes him as "The first colored priest in the United States".

In 2012 the Catholic Church granted Father Augustus the title Servant of God. His cause for canonization advanced further in 2019 when he was given the title Venerable in recognition of having lived a life of heroic virtue.

"Today we can look back at the priestly career of Augustus Tolton and recognize the courage and the faith of

[23] Cyprian Davis, O.S.B., *The History of Black Catholics in the United States* (Chestnut Ridge, N.Y.: Crossroad, 1990), 160.

[24] Hemesath, *From Slave to Priest*, 184–85.

[25] Ibid., 184–85.

[26] Ibid., 184–85.

a man who persevered in his vocation despite insuperable obstacles and opposition", reflects Davis. "He was a pastor, first and last, and justly merits the title of father of all the African American priests who would come after him."[27]

---

[27] Ibid., 162.

DIANE NASH

*Overcoming Injustice with
Truth and Nonviolence*

Early in the morning of April 19, 1960, segregationists bombed the home of Nashville, Tennessee lawyer Z. Alexander Looby, who since February had defended college students arrested in sit-ins promoting the desegregation of lunch counters.[1]

Although the blast destroyed the front of the house and nearly 150 windows at a nearby medical college, the Black civil rights lawyer and his wife escaped unharmed. The racist attack spurred a silent march of more than three thousand students through the town to City Hall led by Fisk University student Diane Nash and the Reverend C.T. Vivian, a Baptist minister.[2] There, outside on the steps, they met Mayor Ben West, whom the Reverend Fisk denounced for not doing more to prevent the escalating violence aimed at stopping the peaceful protests. Soft-spoken but direct, twenty-one-year-old Nash then asked a penetrating question. "Mayor West," she said, "do you feel that it's wrong

---

[1] Jessica Bliss, "On April 19, 1960, the Bombing of a Civil Rights Attorney's Home Set Off a Protest like Few Had Seen in Nashville", *The Tennessean (Nashville)*, April 18, 2020, tennessean.com/story/news/politics/2020/04/19/nashville-civil-rights-protest-april-1960-after-lawyer-z-alexander-looby-bom bing/4807161002/.

[2] Bliss, "April 19, 1960".

to discriminate against a person solely on the basis of his race or color?"

To the surprise of all, West answered yes. The elated marchers applauded.[3] "I tried as best I could to answer frankly and honestly", West recalled in the 1987 documentary series *Eyes on the Prize: America's Civil Rights Years 1954–1965.* "It was a moral question . . . one that a man has to answer, not a politician."[4]

The encounter was a turning point for the student arm of the civil rights movement as three weeks later, Nashville became the first Southern city to desegregate lunch counters. It also established Nash as a key leader of the student movement.[5]

Diane Judith Nash was born May 15, 1938, in Chicago, Illinois, where she grew up in a Black, middle-class Catholic family. She attended both parochial and public schools before graduating from Hyde Park High School in 1956. Remarkably pretty with striking green eyes, she participated in beauty contests as a teen, and at one time she considered becoming a religious sister.[6]

She attended Howard University in Washington, D.C., for two years before transferring to Nashville's Fisk University in 1959. There in the South, she experienced racial segregation for the first time. Being treated as a second-class cit-

---

[3] Lynne Olson, *Freedom's Daughters: The Unsung Heroines of the Civil Rights Movement from 1830–1970* (New York: Scribner, 2001), 159.

[4] *Eyes on the Prize: America's Civil Rights Years (1954–1965)*, documentary series produced by Blackside, Inc., 1987, transcript, shoppbs.pbs.org/wgbh/amex/eyesontheprize/about/pt_103.html.

[5] *Eyes on the Prize.* See also Olson, *Freedom's Daughters*, 159–60.

[6] Meredith Worthen, "Diane Nash Biography", *Biography*, July 9, 2020, biography.com/activist/diane-nash. See also Olson, *Freedom's Daughters*, 153.

izen shocked her and made her determined to seek change.[7] "I was looking forward in college to really expanding myself and growing", Nash recalled in *Eyes on the Prize*. "And that played quite a part when I got to Nashville and why I so keenly resented segregation and not being allowed to do basic kinds of things like eating at restaurants in the ten-cent stores, even. So, you know, I really felt stifled and shut in very unfairly."[8]

In searching out people who were working to stop racial injustice, Nash met the Reverend Jim Lawson, a Methodist minister who was teaching about the nonviolent resistance of Mohandas Gandhi near the Fisk University campus. Although she was initially skeptical, Nash liked the way the method challenged injustice and felt Lawson's group was the only group doing so. Her appreciation grew as she learned the practice is based on upholding truth and proceeding respectfully to transform hatred and injustice with love and forgiveness.[9]

"We have decided that if there is to be suffering in this revolution—which is really what the movement is, a revolution—we will take the suffering upon ourselves and never inflict it upon our fellow man, because we respect him and recognize the God within him", Nash explained, addressing the 1961 National Catholic Conference for Interracial Justice.[10] Convinced of the power of nonviolent resistance

[7] Worthen, "Diane Nash". See also Olson, *Freedom's Daughters*, 154.

[8] *Eyes on the Prize*.

[9] Olson, *Freedom's Daughters*, 154–55.

[10] Diane Nash, "Address to the National Catholic Conference for Interracial Justice", August 25, 1961, Detroit, Michigan, awpc.cattcenter.iastate.edu/201 9/08/09/address-to-the-national-catholic-conference-for-interracial-justice-au gust-25-1961/.

after experiencing it in action, Nash embraced it as a lifelong practice.[11]

While serving as chair of the Student Central Committee that organized the Nashville sit-ins, Nash also took part in the founding of the Student Nonviolent Coordinating Committee, which took place in April 1960 in Raleigh, North Carolina.[12] Like the SCC, an outgrowth of the Reverend Lawson's workshops, SNCC (pronounced *snick*) comprised young people committed to nonviolent, direct-action tactics. In 1961, Nash stepped in to coordinate the famed Freedom Rides when they were on the verge of ending after violent attacks in Anniston and Birmingham, Alabama.[13]

Organized by James Farmer, head of the Congress of Racial Equality, another group dedicated to nonviolent activism, thirteen Freedom Riders (Black and white, male and female) left Washington, D.C., on May 4 to travel by bus through southern states to arrive May 17 in New Orleans, Louisiana. The riders aimed to challenge segregation in interstate bus travel and terminals. On May 14, one bus was firebombed and its escaping passengers attacked by a mob in Anniston, while riders of the other bus were dragged off and beaten by the Ku Klux Klan in Birmingham. The assaults halted the journey. But Nash was adamant that violence would not have the last word. She contacted Farmer and immediately recruited new riders to continue the pilgrimage.[14]

Word quickly reached John Seigenthaler, assistant to Attorney General Robert F. Kennedy, who called Nash at the

[11] *Eyes on the Prize.*
[12] Olson, *Freedom's Daughters*, 155–56.
[13] Ibid., 184.
[14] Ibid., 183–84.

request of his boss and President John F. Kennedy to tell her to stop her people from resuming the Freedom Rides. His pleas fell on deaf ears. "Soon I was shouting, 'Young woman, do you understand what you're doing? . . . Do you understand you're gonna get somebody killed?'" Seigenthaler recalled in the 2010 documentary film *Freedom Riders*. "There's a pause, and she said, 'Sir, you should know, we all signed our last wills and testaments last night before they left. We know someone will be killed. But we cannot let violence overcome nonviolence.'"[15]

Nash was then elected coordinator of the Freedom Rides, which continued into the fall. The rides resulted in a win for the civil rights movement when the Interstate Commerce Commission outlawed segregated bus travel and terminals on November 1, 1961.[16] Just prior to the ruling, Nash was named head of direct-action campaigns for SNCC, which now also included voter registration.[17]

Earlier in 1961, Nash and three other SNCC leaders had spent a month in jail in Rock Hill, South Carolina, after being arrested at a sit-in and adopting a "jail, no bail" stance. Their actions aimed to show support for the Rock Hill Nine, student activists who demanded to be jailed rather than pay bail to protest the injustice of their sit-in arrests and fines. Nash and others had previously used the tactic during the Nashville sit-ins.[18]

[15] *Freedom Riders*, produced by Public Broadcasting Service, American Experience, 2011, pbs.org/wgbh/americanexperience/films/freedomriders/#transcript.

[16] Thaddeus Morgan, "How Freedom Rider Diane Nash Risked Her Life to Desegregate the South", *History*, March 8, 2018, updated January 27, 2021, history.com/news/diane-nash-freedom-rider-civil-rights-movement.

[17] Olson, *Freedom's Daughters*, 198.

[18] Ibid., 158–60.

Nash would also refuse to pay bail in 1962 in Jackson, Mississippi. Instead, she surrendered herself to a two-year jail term for a conviction the previous November of "contributing to the delinquency of minors" by teaching nonviolent resistance to youth. In an open letter stating her position, Nash, who was now married to fellow activist James Bevel and was several months pregnant with their first child, wrote: "I believe that if I go to jail now, it may help hasten that day when my child and all children will be free— not only on the day of their birth, but for all their lives." The judge, perhaps fearing a public relations fiasco, never pursued the sentence. Rather, Nash only served ten days on a contempt of court charge for refusing to move from the white-only section of the courtroom.[19]

Nash had left college in 1961 to work for SNCC and for the Southern Christian Leadership Conference, then headed by the Reverend Martin Luther King Jr. In 1963, she and her husband helped organize the Birmingham, Alabama, desegregation campaign. That year, President Kennedy named Nash to a national committee that paved the way for the Civil Rights Act of 1964. In 1965, she and her husband were organizers of the Selma voting rights movement and of the Selma to Montgomery marches that led to the passing of the Voting Rights Act that year.

Nash and Bevel, who then had two children together, divorced in 1968, and Nash never remarried. She returned to Chicago, where she worked in real estate and fair housing advocacy.[20] She was active in the antiwar movement and

[19] Ibid., 212.
[20] "Diane Nash", Archives of Women's Political Communication, *Iowa State University*, accessed November 8, 2023, awpc.catt center.iastate.edu/direc tory/diane-nash/.

taught the principles of nonviolence. She is the recipient of numerous awards, including the Presidential Medal of Freedom and two honorary degrees from Fisk University and the University of Notre Dame.

"With unmistakable courage and unshakeable courage and leadership, Diane Nash shaped some of the most important civil rights efforts in American history", President Joe Biden said in presenting her with the Medal of Freedom in Washington, D.C., on July 7, 2022. "Yet she is the first to say the medal is shared with hundreds of thousands of patriotic Americans who sacrificed so much for the cause of liberty and justice for all."[21]

---

[21] Joe Biden, "Remarks by President Biden at Presentation of the Presidential Medal of Freedom", July 7, 2022, White House, Washington, D.C., The White House, whitehouse.gov/briefing-room/speeches-remarks/2022/07/07/remarks-by-president-biden-at-presentation-of-the-presidential-medal-of-freedom/.

III
HOPE

DEFINING HOPE

For Christians, success and productivity are not enough. Striving, straining, self-sacrifice, and hard work are not enough either. Perseverance alone will not satisfy the soul. Life, even when it is strenuous, must be full of *joy*. "Rejoice in the Lord always," Saint Paul commands the Philippians. "Again I will say, Rejoice" (Phil 4:4). Saint John explains that his whole motivation for writing his first letter—which we now consider Scripture—is so "that our joy may be complete" (1 Jn 1:4). Shortly before his arrest, Jesus prophesies to his apostles, "I will see you again and your hearts will rejoice, and no one will take your joy from you" (Jn 16:22). From the earliest days of Christianity, joy has been considered one of the fruits of the Holy Spirit, a sign of God's abiding presence in one's life (see Gal 5:22–23; *CCC* 1832).

Yet when life crowds up with struggles and disappointments, how can we be genuinely happy? The saints have long known the secret: *hope*. Hope, which the Catholic Church calls a "theological virtue" (*CCC* 1817–1819), allows people to experience in their hearts the joy of a healed world, of justice and unending love, even though this "seed," which Jesus planted, has not yet fully matured. If the promise of the upcoming weekend can color your Friday with fun and excitement, how much more can God's promise to "make all things new" (Rev 21:5)—a work he has already begun—lighten the dark corners of a Christian's

life. Pope Benedict XVI defines virtue of hope as the certainty that "I am definitively loved and whatever happens to
me—I am awaited by this Love. And so my life is good."[1]
Through the eyes of hope, a Christian such as Servant
of God Julia Greeley, born a slave, could marvel at the
beauty in every child, whether rich or poor, and spend
her life preaching the cheerful news that *we* are all God's
own children, in spite of all mockery. Hope led the former
Lakota medicine man Nicholas Black Elk, who felt a call
to serve as a Catholic catechist, to work for decades among
a people crushed by war and conquest, teaching them not
about blame or revenge, but about the creative power of
Christ, "He Who Makes Live". Christian hope energized
Sister Norma Pimentel, M.J., to respond to the hideous
conditions at the U.S.-Mexico border by building a clean,
safe, and dignified center for migrants—a sign of maternal
compassion that offers refugees a glimmer, however small,
of God's infinitely tender love.

French poet Charles Péguy, a Catholic who died in battle during World War I, calls hope the most powerful of
all virtues. "Hope sees what has not yet been and what
will be," he writes. "She loves what has not yet been and
what will be."[2] As we will see in the stories of Julia Greeley, Nicholas Black Elk, Mother Teresa, and Sister Norma
Pimentel, hope brings joy in the present, but it does so
by urging us forward. This is why Saint Thomas Aquinas
could call hope *motum sive protensionem*—"a movement or
a stretching forth".[3] Christ calls us not to happy compla-

---

[1] Benedict XVI, encyclical letter *Spe Salvi* (November 30, 2011), no. 3.

[2] Charles Péguy, *The Portal of the Mystery of Hope*, trans. David C. Schindler,
Jr. (New York: Continuum, 2005), 9.

[3] *Summa Theologiae* II-II, q. 17, art. 3.

cency, but to jubilant action, walking ever closer to the light of day we spy at the mouth of the cave—and taking others along with us.

CHURCH DOCUMENTS ON HOPE

from U.S. Conference of Catholic Bishops, *Love Thy Neighbor as Thyself (Abridged)* (2014)

The theological virtue of hope is not the same as wishing for the impossible. Christian hope stirs up in us the desire that God's kingdom [will] come, here and in eternity. We place our trust in the promises of Christ and rely on his grace rather than on our own strength.

It would be naive to think that racism will disappear overnight. . . . But change will come if we remain constant and never lose sight of the goal. The goal is visible when we see with the eyes of Christ, for our hope of ultimate victory is the Lord who desires that we be one in him.[1]

from Pope Benedict XVI, *Caritas in Veritate* (2009)

Charity is at the heart of the Church's social doctrine . . . for the Church, instructed by the Gospel, charity is everything because as Saint John teaches (cf. 1 Jn 4:8, 16) and as I recalled in my first encyclical Letter, *God Is Love* (*Deus Caritas Est*): "everything has its origin in God's love, everything

---

[1] United States Conference of Catholic Bishops, *Love Thy Neighbor as Thyself: U.S. Catholic Bishops Speak Against Racism*, abridged ed. (Washington, D.C.: United States Conference of Catholic Bishops, 2014), usccb.org/issues -and-action/cultural-diversity/african-american/upload/14-026-love-thy-neig hbor.pdf.

is shaped by it, everything is directed towards it." Love is God's greatest gift to humanity, it is his promise and our hope.[2]

from Pope Benedict XVI, *Spe Salvi* (2007)

"Hope" . . . is a key word in Biblical faith—so much so that in several passages the words "faith" and "hope" seem interchangeable. . . . We see as a distinguishing mark of Christians the fact that they have a future: it is not that they know the details of what awaits them, but they know in general terms that their life will not end in emptiness. Only when the future is certain as a positive reality does it become possible to live the present as well. . . . Christianity was not only "good news"—the communication of a hitherto unknown content. In our language we would say: the Christian message was not only "informative" but "performative." That means: the Gospel is not merely a communication of things that can be known—it is one that makes things happen and is life-changing. The dark door of time, of the future, has been thrown open. The one who has hope lives differently; the one who hopes has been granted the gift of a new life. . . .

Faith is the "substance" of things hoped for; the proof of things not seen [Heb 11:1]. . . . Faith is not merely a personal reaching out towards things to come that are still totally absent: it gives us something. It gives us even now something of the reality we are waiting for, and this present reality constitutes for us a "proof" of the things that are

[2] Pope Benedict XVI, encyclical letter *Caritas in Veritate* (June 29, 2009), vatican.va/content/benedict-xvi/en/encyclicals/documents/hf_ben-xvi_enc_20090629_caritas-in-veritate.html.

still unseen. Faith draws the future into the present, so that it is no longer simply a "not yet." The fact that this future exists changes the present; the present is touched by the future reality, and thus the things of the future spill over into those of the present and those of the present into those of the future.[3]

[3] Pope Benedict XVI, encyclical letter *Spe Salvi* (November 30, 2007), vatican.va/content/benedict-xvi/en/encyclicals/documents/hf_ben-xvi_enc_20071130_spe-salvi.html.

JULIA GREELEY

Denver's Apostle of the Sacred Heart
and Angel of Charity

The only person buried at Denver's century-old Cathedral Basilica of the Immaculate Conception is a former slave.

Servant of God Julia Greeley was a Catholic convert laywoman who, through faith, rose above the racism and injustice she experienced as a poor, uneducated, ex-slave, answering those wrongs with heroic acts of charity, which brought comfort and hope to their beneficiaries. "Old Julia" was so beloved in her adopted city that upon her death in 1918, people from all walks of life filed past her body for five hours as it lay in state at a small chapel to pay their respects.[1]

Born into slavery between 1833 and 1848 near Hannibal, Missouri—Julia did not know her birth year—as a child she lost an eye to a whip while she clung to her mother, who was being beaten by a slave master. The blinded, weeping

---

[1] Blaine Burkey, O.F.M. Cap., ed., *In Secret Service of the Sacred Heart: Life and Virtues of Julia Greeley*, 3rd expanded ed. (Denver: Julia Greeley Guild, 2021), 11, 12, 14. This citation and many following refer to information in the obituary reprinted in Burkey's book: "Highest Honor Ever Paid to Dead Laic Here Goes to Negress", *Denver Catholic Register*, June 13, 1918. A facsimile of the obituary may be found at the Archdiocese of Denver Digital Repository, (archives.archden.org/islandora/object/archden%3A2859/datastream/OBJ/view), and its text at the site of the Julia Greeley Guild, (juliagreeley.org/index.php/obituary/).

eye was a lasting mark of the cruelty she had endured.[2] "Yet, she refused to hate", noted historian Tom Noel. "The scar marred her face but not her soul."[3]

Freed in 1865 by Missouri's Emancipation Proclamation Act, Julia worked over the years as a domestic for families in Missouri, Colorado, Wyoming, and New Mexico. In about 1878, she arrived in Denver, which remained her home for most of her adult life. There, she initially worked for Julia Gilpin, a Catholic and wife of Colorado's first territorial governor, William Gilpin. She credited her conversion to Catholicism, in 1880 at Denver's Sacred Heart Church, to Mrs. Gilpin. Thereafter, she was a daily Mass attendee who called the Eucharist her "breakfast".[4]

Julia became known for her devotion to the Sacred Heart of Jesus, symbol of Christ's sacrificial love for humanity and victory over sin and death. Each first Friday of the month, she trekked to all twenty of Denver's fire stations to give Sacred Heart badges and Apostleship of Prayer pamphlets to the firemen, Catholic or not, because their jobs were so dangerous. Because of her rampant arthritis, her monthly twenty-two-mile pilgrimage was surely painful.[5]

Although Julia couldn't read the leaflets she gave out, she knew they encouraged prayer and offering one's day to Christ. She called them "tickets to heaven". Her fervent evangelization compelled her parish priests to christen her "the most zealous Apostle of the Sacred Heart".[6]

[2] Burkey, *Secret Service*, 66, 79, 113–14, 138.

[3] Tom Noel, "Noel: Julia Greeley, 'Angel of Charity'", *The Denver Post*, February 14, 2014, denverpost.com/2014/02/14/noel-julia-greeley-angel-of-charity/.

[4] Burkey, *Secret Service*, 13–14, 19, 79–84, 114, 139.

[5] Ibid., 12–13, 54–56, 135.

[6] Ibid., 12–13, 63.

Besides fostering devotion to the Sacred Heart, in 1901 Julia further sought to live the Gospel by becoming a Third Order Franciscan. When she died, she was buried in a secular Franciscan habit.[7]

After Julia's service with the Gilpins ended in 1883, she began doing odd jobs cooking, cleaning, and caring for children. She was a familiar sight on Denver streets in her secondhand clothing, floppy hat, and oversized shoes, often pulling a red wagon or carrying a gunnysack. These she filled with necessities that she bought, found, or begged to give to the needy. She frequently delivered these goods at night to avoid embarrassing the recipients, particularly if they were white.[8]

At one point, she gave up her own burial plot to save an ex-slave from being buried in the potter's field. Her astonishing generosity, despite her paltry income of ten to twelve dollars a month, won her the title Denver's Angel of Charity.[9]

Despite her tireless support of Sacred Heart Church, Julia faced prejudice at her parish from some of wealthy faithful. Her tiny pew was at the foot of a huge crucifix near the altar, where she was visible to all. Complaints were made about her shabby appearance at High Mass. Hearing this, Julia offered to attend another Mass. But the pastor, Jesuit Father Edward Barry, swiftly closed the debate, declaring, "Julia can sit any place in this church she wants to."[10]

It was said Julia's smile was unforgettable. Children made her smile. Julia delighted in them. In the only known photo of Julia, taken in 1916, she is holding one of her precious

---

[7] Ibid., 15, 31–33, 113.

[8] Ibid., 3, 8, 10–11, 13–14, 25, 62.

[9] Ibid., 9, 14, 29, 72, 75.

[10] Ibid., 52.

charges, seven-month-old Marjorie A. Urquhart, whose birth she had predicted to the child's mother upon learning that the then-childless woman had lost an infant to an agonizing death ten years before, and that it was not possible for her to have more children.[11]

"There will be a little white angel running around this house. I will pray and you'll see," Julia reportedly prophesied. When indeed Marjorie was born the next year, Julia provided childcare.[12]

While on her way to morning Mass on June 7, 1918, Julia collapsed and was taken to a friend's house across from the church rectory. The friend quickly sent for a priest, who gave Julia Last Rites. She was then taken to the hospital, where she died. That it was the feast of the Sacred Heart seemed providential to those who knew Julia—a final grace given to her whose loving service testified to a heart like that of her beloved Christ.[13]

Immediately, many expressed a desire to see the saintly woman canonized. The quest grew over the years. In 2016, the Denver archdiocese opened Julia's cause for canonization, allowing her to be called Servant of God. In 2017, her remains were exhumed from a local cemetery and reinterred at the Cathedral Basilica. In 2021, the Congregation for the Causes of Saints issued a decree approving the validity of the investigation into her life and devotion to her.[14]

Reflecting on the Sacred Heart, Bishop Donald Hying wrote: "The death and resurrection of Christ is the gentle yet powerful absorption, deflection and transformation of violence into love, sin into grace, hatred into forgiveness

[11] Ibid., 14, 26, 43–44.
[12] Ibid., 26, 43–44.
[13] Ibid., 5–6, 11–15, 23–24.
[14] Ibid., 131, 134–35, 137.

and death into life. . . . The triumph of the Sacred Heart is the ultimate victory of love."[15]

By the time Julia died, her Beloved's Heart had become her own. Her love transcended the racism, violence, and cruelty she had faced. Today, as then, her life shines as a ray of hope: she spoke love to hate and triumphed.

[15] Donald J. Hying "Understanding the Devotion to the Sacred Heart of Jesus and What It Means", *Simply Catholic*, accessed November 8, 2023, simplycatholic.com/why-the-sacred-heart/.

NICK BLACK ELK AND FAMILY
CATHOLIC CATECHIST.

NICHOLAS BLACK ELK

From Medicine Man to Catechist

When Black Elk, an Oglala Lakota, was nine years old, he had a great vision that led to his vocation to be a spiritual and physical healer for his people. His vision was made famous when author-poet John G. Neihardt shared it in the 1932 book *Black Elk Speaks*. The story ends with the tragic 1890 Wounded Knee Massacre of some three hundred Lakota people by U.S. Army soldiers and a somber lament composed by Neihardt but attributed to Black Elk: "A people's dream died there. It was a beautiful dream."[1]

When interviewed by Neihardt, Black Elk was in his late sixties and partially blind. The book, however, only includes Black Elk's youth and young adulthood. Left out of his "life story" is the fact that Black Elk had been a Catholic catechist for decades and was known among his people for bringing hope, healing, and new life in Christ to them.

Disappointed that Neihardt had not included his Catholicism, Black Elk wrote a letter to his people in 1934 saying: "Listen, I speak some true words. A white man made a book and told what I had spoken of olden times, but the new times he left out. So I speak again, a last word. . . . In the last thirty years I am different from what the white man

---

[1] Damian Costello, *Black Elk: Colonialism and Lakota Catholicism* (Maryknoll, N.Y.: Orbis Books, 2005), 7–9.

wrote about me. I am a Christian."[2] In fact, he was a pro-
lific evangelist. When he died at eighty-seven in 1950, he
was credited with bringing more than four hundred people
into the Church and serving as godfather to more than a
hundred.[3]

Black Elk was born in July 1863 along the Little Pow-
der River in present-day Wyoming.[4] His father, grandfather,
and great-grandfather were all medicine men. His father was
a cousin of the famed Lakota chief and war leader Crazy
Horse. Black Elk had his great vision in 1872 on what is now
called Black Elk Peak in South Dakota. In another vision
in 1881, his vocation was reaffirmed and expanded to "use
his gift to 'help mankind' ", after which he was recognized
as a medicine man.[5]

In his youth, Black Elk hunted buffalo with his father
in Montana and Canada.[6] In 1876, when just thirteen, he
fought in the legendary Indian victory at the Battle of Little
Bighorn. In 1889 he took part in the ghost dance movement,

[2] Nicholas Black Elk, Letter to Holy Rosary Mission, Pine Ridge, South
Dakota, January 26, 1934, rapidcitydiocese.org/wp-content/uploads/2019/08
/1934-1-24.pdf.
[3] Patrick McNamara, "Nicholas Black Elk: This Sioux Medicine Man May
Be Recognized as a Saint", Aleteia, November 17, 2017, aleteia.org/2017/11/
16/nicholas-black-elk-this-sioux-medicine-man-may-be-recognized-as-a-saint/.
[4] There is conflicting information about the month and year of Black Elk's
birth, which are said to be July or December and from 1858 to 1866. Neihardt
used 1863, and that is consistent with the Pine Ridge census of 1900. Black
Elk's daughter Lucy said he was born in July; she explained that December
was the month of his baptism or spiritual birthday. See also Michael F. Steltenkamp, S.J., Nicholas Black Elk: Medicine Man, Missionary, Mystic (Norman,
Okla.: University of Oklahoma Press, 2009), 15–16; and Costello, Black
Elk, 5.
[5] Steltenkamp, Nicholas Black Elk, 51.
[6] Ibid., 41.

which aimed to revive Native American culture. In 1890, he was injured in the Wounded Knee Massacre, where he tried to move people to safety.[7]

From 1886 to 1889, Black Elk had toured Europe, initially as part of Buffalo Bill's Wild West show, which included a command performance for Queen Victoria; he then performed for a time with Mexican Joe, Shelley's western show. While in Europe, he was impressed with the great cathedrals and the Christian piety of those who worshiped in them.[8]

Upon his return to the Pine Ridge Reservation in South Dakota from Europe, Black Elk carried out a healing ministry and worked as a store clerk.[9] In 1892, he married Katie War Bonnet. She was Catholic, and their three sons were baptized into the Catholic faith. Black Elk's firstborn son, William, died in 1895. Six years later, Katie died.

Black Elk converted to Catholicism on December 6, 1904. It was the feast of Saint Nicholas, and he took Nicholas William as his baptismal name. A year after his conversion, he married a widow with two daughters, Anna Brings White, with whom he had two sons and a daughter. Their children, too, were baptized Catholic. Sadly, before Anna died in 1941, she and Black Elk had lost four of their seven children.

Biographer Damian Costello notes that when Black Elk converted, he "embraced a different way of healing. Utilizing his abilities to memorize Scripture and speak persuasively, he became a missionary disciple. He served as a catechist,

---

[7] McNamara, "Nicholas Black Elk".
[8] Steltenkamp, *Nicholas Black Elk*, 56–57.
[9] Ibid., 51, 60.

which in his community functioned much like a permanent deacon does today."[10]

Historian Patrick McNamara observes that when Black Elk became Catholic, "he also discovered a new calling. He told a friend, 'I want to be a catechist the rest of my life.'"[11] Indeed, he served as a catechist for more than forty years.

A tool Black Elk used in catechizing was a colorful pictorial ladder catechism called the Two Roads Map, which featured the Good Red Road and the Black Road of Difficulties. In addition to preparing people for the sacraments, holding Communion services, baptizing, conducting burial services, and preaching—his dynamic preaching led one priest to dub him "a second Saint Paul"[12]—he was a tireless evangelizer who traveled to other states and reservations, undaunted by prejudice, to announce the good news about Jesus, whom Lakota call Wanikiya, meaning "He Who Makes Live".[13]

"For Black Elk, Jesus and his new life were the answer to a collapsing world: Only he can fully heal the Earth, bring back the dead and explain how to make sense of the newcomers", wrote Costello. "The buffalo were killed. The old way of life was destroyed. The Lakota people were impris-

---

[10] Damian Costello, "Nicholas Black Elk: Prophet to Lakota a Sign of Hope Today", *Catholic Philly*, April 15, 2019, catholicphilly.com/2019/04/comment aries/nicholas-black-elk-prophet-to-lakota-a-sign-of-hope-today/.

[11] McNamara, "Nicholas Black Elk".

[12] Ibid.

[13] Ibid. See also Laurie Hallstrom, "Black Elk, Cause for Canonization to Open", *West River Catholic*, October 2017, rapidcitydiocese.org/wp-content/uploads/2017/10/WRC-oct-17-reduced.pdf; and Peter Jesserer Smith, "Black Elk: Future Patron Saint and Model for Instituted Lay Catechists?", *National Catholic Register*, August 18, 2021, ncregister.com/news/black-elk-future-patron-saint-and-model-for-instituted-lay-catechists.

oned on reservations and forcibly reprogrammed."[14] Despite that cataclysmic situation and his personal losses and sufferings, adds Costello, "Black Elk learned to live a vibrant life of hope. . . . With the skill of an artist, he wove seemingly different strands into one beautiful life: He preached the Gospel, worked to save the old ways and built bridges across artificial divisions that separate us into warring tribes. Black Elk once healed the sick with sacred songs; with his baptism he became a missionary disciple of life, radiating the healing love of Wanikiya into a broken world."[15]

Revered among the Lakota as a holy man, Black Elk successfully "bridged the gap between traditional native spirituality and Catholicism", Deacon Marlon Leneaugh, Native Ministry director for the Rapid City Diocese, told the *West River Catholic* newspaper. "He showed his people that you did not have to choose between the two, you could be both. . . . To him it was together—praying to the one God."[16]

Not long before his death, the ailing Nicholas Black Elk told his daughter Lucy he thought God might send a sign after he died to affirm that his soul was at rest. "Maybe God will show something", he said, "which will tell of his mercy." On August 19, 1950, Nicholas Black Elk received Last Rites before dying in his home in Pine Ridge. Costello reports that "both Lakota and Jesuits observed strange lights in the sky the night of his wake."[17]

"The sky was just one bright illumination", said William Siehr, a Jesuit brother at Holy Rosary Mission since 1938,

[14] Costello, "Nicholas Black Elk".
[15] Ibid.
[16] Hallstrom, "Black Elk".
[17] Costello, *Colonialism*, 13.

describing the flashing northern lights. "I never saw anything so magnificent."[18]

"Everything looked miracle-like", said John Lone Goose, who worked with Black Elk as a fellow catechist. "I know God sent those beautiful objects to shine on that old missionary. Maybe the Holy Spirit shined upon him because he was such a holy man."[19]

The canonization process for Nicholas Black Elk was formally opened by Rapid City Bishop Robert Gruss on October 21, 2017, a year after grandchildren of the holy man presented a petition to the bishop requesting a sainthood cause be initiated. With the process officially begun, Nicholas Black Elk bears the title Servant of God, and people may ask for his intercession. Three other major steps follow before a person may be declared a saint, two of which require a miracle credited to the person's intercession.

At the Mass closing the diocesan phase of Black Elk's canonization cause (after which information about his life was sent to Rome for review to determine whether he lived a life of heroic virtue), Bishop Gruss ended his homily by saying, "May [Black Elk] continue to inspire many others to walk the good red road as he did, offering a way forward in hope—a better path for all. Nicholas Black Elk, pray for us."[20]

[18] Ibid., 13.
[19] Ibid., 13.
[20] Robert D. Gruss, "Homily for the Mass Concluding the Diocesan Phase of the Cause for Beatification and Canonization of Servant of God Nicholas William Black Elk, Sr.", June 25, 2019, St. Agnes Church, Manderson, South Dakota, blackelkcanonization.com/wp-content/uploads/2019/10/Mass-for-t he-Conclusion-of-the-Diocesan-Phase-of-the-Cause-for-Beatification-and-Ca nonization-of-Servant-of-God-Nicholas-W.pdf.

SAINT TERESA OF CALCUTTA

"Come, Be My Light"

On September 10, 1946, Mother Teresa was on her way to a retreat in the Himalayan foothills, hundreds of miles north of Calcutta (now Kolkata), where she was principal at a girls' school. On the train, the Loreto nun interiorly heard Christ calling her to a new mission. Thereafter, she would refer to the experience as "the call within the call".[1] "It was a call within my vocation", she later explained. "It was a second calling. It was a vocation to give up even Loreto where I was very happy and to go out in the streets to serve the poorest of the poor."[2]

Of Albanian descent, she was thirty-six and had entered the Irish-based Loreto Sisters seventeen years earlier to be a missionary in India. Now Christ was asking her to establish a new religious order, the Missionaries of Charity, to serve the most destitute. They would take God's love—his light and hope—to the marginalized.

"Come, come, carry me into the holes of the poor", Mother Teresa heard Christ say. "Come, be my light."[3]

---

[1] Brian Kolodiejchuk, M.C., *Mother Teresa: Come Be My Light* (New York: Doubleday, 2007), 40.

[2] Malcolm Muggeridge, *Something Beautiful for God* (New York: Ballantine Books, 1971), 65.

[3] Kolodiejchuk, *Mother Teresa*, 44.

The purpose of the Missionaries of Charity, the founder would explain, was to "satiate the thirst of Jesus by serving him in the poorest of the poor".[4] In Matthew's Gospel, Christ identifies himself with the hungry, thirsty, naked, sick, and imprisoned and with the stranger, asserting: "As you did it to one of the least of these my brethren, you did it to me" (Mt 25:40). Mother Teresa often summarized the Gospel on one hand by reciting a word for each finger: "You-Did-It-To-Me."[5] In serving the "least of these", the Missionaries of Charity would also be serving Christ. Additionally, they would be satisfying Christ's cry "I thirst" from the Cross. For Mother Teresa, Christ's thirst expressed not only universal human need, but also "his longing for the love and salvation of every human person".[6]

Mother Teresa's profound love and faith made her open and receptive to the life-changing call she experienced on the train. That faith had been primarily fostered by her mother and her parish as she was growing up. She was born Gonxha Agnes Bojaxhiu on August 26, 1910, in Skopje, now the capital of Macedonia. The youngest of five children, two of whom died in infancy, she had an older sister and brother. Her father, Nikola, was a merchant who died suddenly when she was eight—some suspected he was poisoned by political enemies. His death left the family struggling financially for

[4] Ibid., 40.

[5] Brandon Vogt, "Jesus in His Most Distressing Disguise", *Word on Fire*, September 5, 2014, wordonfire.org/articles/jesus-in-his-most-distressing-disguise/. See also Tommy Tighe, "Dorothy Day, Mother Teresa and the 5-Finger Gospel", *Aleteia*, April 21, 2017, aleteia.org/2017/04/21/dorothy-day-mother-teresa-and-the-5-finger-gospel/.

[6] Kolodiejchuk, *Mother Teresa*, 4. See also James Martin, S.J., "Teresa of Jesus", in *Mother Teresa: The Life and Works of a Modern Saint*, ed. Richard Lacayo (New York: Time Books, 2012), 24.

a few years. Her mother, Drana, was a devout and charitable woman who opened their home to the poor at mealtimes. It was she who taught Gonxha ("Flower Bud") the five-word Gospel summary: You-Did-It-To-Me.[7]

At age twelve, Gonxha felt a call to serve the poor and to be a missionary. At eighteen, she went to Ireland to enter the Sisters of Loreto in Dublin, with the intention of serving at their mission in India. She took the religious name Teresa after Saint Thérèse of Lisieux, whose "little way" to holiness entails doing small tasks with great love. Within months, she departed for India for a two-year novitiate in Darjeeling. In 1931, as Sister Teresa, she was assigned to teach at Saint Mary's High School in Calcutta. Run by the Loreto Sisters, the school taught girls from poor and middle-class Bengali families. In 1937, Sister Teresa professed final vows and in the tradition of Loreto nuns assumed the title "Mother". She continued teaching geography and history at Saint Mary's and in 1944 became the school's principal.

It was a sacrifice to leave the Loreto Sisters and her students once permission was granted for her to start the Missionaries of Charity in 1948, two years after experiencing her "call within a call" on the train. But she was certain of Christ's desire. "I knew it was his will, and that I had to follow him", she told journalist Malcolm Muggeridge in 1969. "There was no doubt that it was going to be his work. But I waited for the decision of the Church."[8]

In mid-August 1948 she left the Loreto convent with just five rupees, resolute to depend on God's providence for the means to carry out her ministry. She replaced her former

[7] Tighe, "Dorothy Day".
[8] Muggeridge, *Something Beautiful*, 66.

religious habit with the cheapest sari available, white with a blue border, which she also used to veil her hair. The only item identifying her as a nun was the crucifix pinned on one shoulder. The sari would become the unique habit for the Missionaries of Charity, who commit themselves to dress like, live among, and serve the poorest of the poor.[9]

Mother Teresa's first task was to undergo four months of basic medical training in Patna. That December, she returned to Calcutta, staying temporarily with the Little Sisters of the Poor, and started her ministry in the slums to "the unwanted, the unloved, the uncared for".[10]

On her first day she visited many families and nursed the sick, including an ailing elderly man lying in the street and a starving woman with tuberculosis dying at a marketplace. She soon gathered street children and started an open-air school. As the student body grew, so did volunteers and donations, which quickly enabled her to rent two rooms for the school. "And so the work started growing", she later recalled. "The sisters started coming in 1949. . . . The first 10 girls who came were all students I had taught in the school."[11]

By June 1950, there were a dozen Missionaries of Charity. That October, the congregation was officially recognized by the Vatican. The previous year, Mother Teresa had become a citizen of India.

In 1952 Mother Teresa opened her first Home for the Dying in Calcutta, which provides comfort and dignity to the destitute who would otherwise die alone and abandoned

[9] Martin, "Teresa of Jesus", 24.
[10] "Mother Teresa Biography", *Biography*, updated February 24, 2020, biography.com/religious-figures/mother-teresa.
[11] Muggeridge, *Something Beautiful*, 68, 70.

in the street. It was inspired when the nun rescued one such woman who was "half-eaten by the rats and ants" and took her to a hospital that initially refused her as a hopeless cause.[12] Mother Teresa's insistence that she be treated prevailed. Aware of the extent of street deaths, she then asked for a hospice site from city authorities, which they gave her. Early on, a grateful hospice resident, a formerly worm-infested man who was saved from dying in the gutter, told her, "I have lived like an animal on the street, but I die like an angel, loved and cared for."[13]

After founding the hospice, Mother Teresa opened a home for orphans. She also began caring for lepers and launched mobile health clinics. After ten years of ministry in Calcutta, the Missionaries of Charity were permitted to spread to other parts of India. In 1965, the congregation established its first house outside India, in Venezuela. Thereafter, the Missionaries of Charity quickly spread all over the world.

To best serve the physical and spiritual needs of the poor as her ministry expanded in the sixties through the eighties, Mother Teresa founded the Missionaries of Charity Brothers, contemplative branches of religious sisters and brothers, and a branch of priests. Lay volunteers were eventually consolidated into an international and interreligious association called the Co-workers of Mother Teresa.

As the range of Mother Teresa's work spread, so too did her reputation, primarily in the communities in which she and her sisters served, and in the Church. But in the late sixties and early seventies, she became world famous when

[12] Ibid., 71.

[13] Eileen Egan, *Such a Vision of the Street: Mother Teresa, the Spirit and the Work* (London: Sidgwick & Jackson, 1986), 55.

Muggeridge interviewed her twice for BBC television, then produced a documentary and a book titled with a phrase she often used, "something beautiful for God".[14]

The humble nun was also the recipient of prominent awards, including the 1971 Pope John XXIII Peace Award, the 1979 Nobel Peace Prize, and the 1985 U.S. Presidential Medal of Freedom. Not only did Mother Teresa use the money associated with these awards for those she served, but she convinced the Nobel Committee to waive the awards banquet and donate that money to the poor as well.[15] She was awarded the Nobel Peace Prize for her "work in bringing help to suffering humanity".[16] Calling herself "unworthy", she expressed gratitude for the "gift of recognition of the poorest of the poor of the world" and accepted the award "on their behalf".[17]

Although Mother Teresa faced seemingly insurmountable need when she cared for the poor, the sick, or the disaster-stricken across the globe, she simply did what she could for the person before her, whom she saw as Christ. "Maybe if I had not picked up that one person dying on the street, I would not have picked up the thousands", Mother Teresa often noted. "We must think, Ek (Bengali for 'One'). Ek, Ek. One, One. That is the way to begin."[18]

[14] Ibid., 216.

[15] Mike Nicol, "Mother Teresa", in *Love: The Words and Inspiration of Mother Teresa*, by Mother Teresa of Calcutta (Boulder: Blue Mountain Press, 2007), 19.

[16] The Nobel Prize, "The Nobel Peace Prize 1979", *Nobel Prize*, October 27, 1979, nobelprize.org/prizes/peace/1979/press-release/.

[17] Kathryn Spink, *Mother Teresa: A Complete Authorized Biography* (San Francisco: HarperSanFrancisco, 1997), 167–68.

[18] Eileen Egan, *Prayertimes with Mother Teresa* (New York: Image Books, 1989), 63.

Because of the joy Mother Teresa radiated, the world was astonished to learn years after her death that she had experienced a decades-long "dark night of the soul". The feeling of being separated from God began in 1948 when she started her ministry to the most destitute and, except for a five-week respite, continued until her death in 1997.[19] The revelation came with the 2007 publication of her private letters in *Mother Teresa: Come Be My Light*, edited by Missionary of Charity Father Brian Kolodiejchuk.

With the help of her spiritual director, Jesuit Father Joseph Neuner, Mother Teresa eventually came to see the suffering as part of the spiritual side of her work and integral to it. She understood that "through the darkness she mystically participated in the thirst of Jesus, in his painful and burning longing for love, and she shared in the interior desolation of the poor."[20] "I have come to love the darkness", Mother Teresa reported to Father Neuner in 1961.[21] Her embrace of the darkness deepened, leading her to express to him the following year what Father Kolodiejchuk called a "mission statement": "If I ever become a saint—I will surely be one of 'darkness.' I will continually be absent from heaven—to light the light of those in darkness on earth."[22]

Despite increasing health problems that began with a heart attack in 1983, Mother Teresa continued serving the poor globally and leading her congregation until March 1997,

[19] David Van Biema, "Her Agony", in *Mother Teresa: The Life and Works of a Modern Saint*, ed. Richard Lacayo (New York: Time Books, 2012), 80.

[20] "Mother Teresa of Calcutta (1910–1997)", The Holy See, accessed November 9, 2023, vatican.va/news_services/liturgy/saints/ns_lit_doc_20031 019_madre-teresa_en.html.

[21] Kolodiejchuk, *Mother Teresa*, 208, 214.

[22] Ibid., 1, 230.

when she blessed her newly elected successor. She died that September in Calcutta and was given a state funeral. At the time of her death, there were nearly 4,000 Missionaries of Charity sisters ministering in 610 foundations in 123 nations.[23]

A year after her death, because of her universal recognition as a holy woman and favors reported, Saint John Paul II permitted the opening of her canonization cause, waiving the customary five-year wait. Mother Teresa was beatified on October 19, 2003, after a miracle was credited to her intercession. She was canonized on September 4, 2016, after a second miracle was attributed to her intercession.

"She was truly a witness to hope, an apostle of love and joy", wrote Father Kolodiejchuk, who knew Mother Teresa and served as postulator (researcher for evidence of holiness) for her canonization cause.[24] In *Come Be My Light*, Father Kolodiejchuk shares a story about Mother Teresa that, he testifies, "expresses the heart of her life and mission": While visiting her sisters in Australia, Mother Teresa entered the tin and cardboard shack of an Aborigine man on the outskirts of Bourke and offered to clean it. In cleaning, she found a beautiful dirt-covered lamp the man never lit, as he never had visitors. "Won't you light it if the sisters come to you?" she asked. He said he would. The sisters came and would light the lamp. Eventually, their calls became a quick hello. Two years later, the man sent a message through the sisters: "Tell Mother, my friend, the light she lit in my life is still burning."[25]

---

[23] "Mother Teresa of Calcutta".
[24] Kolodiejchuk, *Mother Teresa*, 4.
[25] Ibid., 339–40.

SISTER NORMA PIMENTEL

Restoring Dignity and Renewing Hope
on the U.S.-Mexico border

She's been called "the pope's favorite nun" since being praised by Pope Francis in a televised virtual meeting in August 2015 for her compassionate work serving thousands of immigrants along the U.S.-Mexico border for some thirty years.

When Missionary of Jesus Sister Norma Pimentel met the pope in person during his visit to New York City the following month, she gave him a portrait she had painted of a Honduran mother and son she had served. It is titled *Tomasito*, after the boy. "I saw in their faces the great pain and suffering they had been through that represents for the most part what all immigrants go through at the border", Sister Pimentel said softly about the beautiful pastel image.[1]

Sister Pimentel's ministry to migrants captured international attention in 2014 when a dramatic rise in the number of unaccompanied children and families from Central America arriving at the Rio Grande Valley on the Texas-Mexico border caused a crisis.[2] "They were in terrible condition",

[1] Sr. Norma Pimentel, M.J.,telephone interview with Roxanne King, January 19, 2022. Quotations from Sister Norma in this chapter are from this interview unless otherwise indicated.

[2] Dara Lind, "The 2014 Central American Migrant Crisis", *Vox*, October 10, 2014, vox.com/2014/10/10/18088638/child-migrant-crisis-unaccompani ed-alien-children-rio-grande-valley-obama-immigration.

Sister Pimentel said of the families. "They had traveled long journeys and had encountered many hardships. The Border Patrol didn't have a facility to provide them with anything other than to process them and immediately release them."

Tragically, due to the overwhelming numbers and lack of facilities, unaccompanied children were sometimes held for days or weeks at Border Patrol processing centers in over-crowded, jail-like conditions until facilities for such children became available.[3] "To visit the detention facility where they were apprehended and processed and seeing the children in those cells was very heartbreaking for me. It was like I had a dagger in my heart when I saw the suffering children with faces full of tears asking me to help them and not being able to remove them from there", Sister Pimentel told *Global Sisters Report*. "That experience has marked me forever. That triggered in me a profound sense of commitment and dedication to make sure that I become that voice for them, that I can be that force that can defend and protect life, especially the immigrants."[4] Fortunately, 90 percent of unaccompanied children were released to relatives that summer.[5]

Sister Pimentel, who had run a refugee shelter for ten years and, as head of Catholic Charities of the Rio Grande

[3] Sr. Norma Pimentel , M.J., Testimony to U.S. Commission on Civil Rights, 2014, *U.S. Commission on Civil Rights*, accessed November 9, 2023, usccr.gov/files/pubs/OIG/Sr._Norma_Pimentel's_130.15_TestimonyUSCommisionCivilRights.pdf.

[4] Soli Salgado and Dan Stockman, "Sr. Norma Pimentel, LCWR Award Recipient, Embraces 'Holy Chaos' of Her Ministry to Migrants", *Global Sisters Report*, August 17, 2019, globalsistersreport.org/ news/ministry-trends/sr-norma-pimentel-lcwr-award-recipient-embraces-holy-chaos-her-ministry.

[5] Lind, "Migrant Crisis". See also Alan Greenblatt, "What's Causing the Latest Immigration Crisis? A Brief Explainer", *NPR*, July 9, 2014, npr.org/2014/07/09/329848538/whats-causing-the-latest-immigration-crisis-a-brief-explainer.

Valley, had a wealth of experience providing emergency assistance, called on people in the community to help establish a respite center at a local Catholic church in McAllen,
Texas. "We used the parish hall at Sacred Heart Church",
she said. "I borrowed it for a couple of days, which turned
into a couple of years. That was our initial start."

After two subsequent moves, the Humanitarian Respite
Center secured its present site across the street from the bus
station, from which many migrants continue their journey
after their release from U.S. Customs and Border Protection. But first they are offered a much-needed rest stop at
the center, which offers relief aid, including a shower, clean
clothes, a meal, water, medical assistance if necessary, and
general information. The ministry has served more than one
hundred fifty thousand migrants of all ages from thirteen
countries.

Most of the migrants are from the Northern Triangle of
Central America—Honduras, Guatemala, and El Salvador—
and are desperately seeking to escape violence and poverty.[6]
They undertake their perilous journey to the United States,
which can include dodging predators ranging from human
traffickers to kidnappers, for the ray of hope their desti
nation holds. "They want Border Patrol to apprehend and
process them", Sister Pimentel said. "They want asylum in
the United States."

Under the Migrant Protection Protocols (also known as
the Remain in Mexico policy) asylum-seekers are given no-
tices to appear in immigration court before being sent back
to Mexico (from which they have crossed into the United

---

[6] Lind, "Migrant Crisis". See also Tom Dart, "Child Migrants at Texas
Border: An Immigration Crisis That's Hardly New", *The Guardian*, July 9,
2014, theguardian.com/world/2014/jul/09/us-immigration-undocumented
-children-texas; and Greenblatt, "Immigration Crisis".

States between port of entry points) to wait for their court hearing. The migrants also face extreme danger there— many are left homeless or stay in squalid tent cities.[7] "They migrate hoping that in the U.S. they will have a chance for their children to be safe, to go to school, to grow up. That's their hope", Sister Pimentel said. "They risk their lives in so many ways. . . . They are people who simply want a chance at life. We should not be afraid of them."

After having traveled for weeks or months constantly on guard for their safety, when the exhausted and often abused or exploited migrants enter the respite center with not much more than what they are wearing, they are welcomed with applause and caring hospitality. The effects of experiencing a sincere inquiry about how they are doing, getting to shower, changing into clean clothes, and filling up on a warm meal is lifegiving and transformative, the nun said. "I see so many fathers drop to their knees and start to cry and pray and give thanks that they are in the presence of people with a welcoming heart. Being able to provide that and to begin to restore their dignity is what starts to happen once they enter the doors of the respite center", Sister Pimentel said. "They are coming hopeful, and our presence gives them hope."

Although the respite center typically sees 100–150 immigrants a day, it can hold up to 1,200 people. "We've seen very low numbers to very high numbers many times since 2014", Sister Pimentel explained. "We never thought we'd

---

[7] "The 'Migrant Protection Protocols': Fact Sheet", *American Immigration Council*, January 7, 2022, americanimmigrationcouncil.org/research/migrant-protection-protocols. See also Sr. Norma Pimentel, M.J., "Opinion: What Biden Can Do for Migrants Stuck in Mexico, Despite MPP", *Washington Post*, September 6, 2021, washingtonpost.com/opinions/2021/09/06/norma-pimentel-mpp-biden-help-migrants/.

reach 1,200 people in 2019, and this past summer (2021) we reached almost 2,000 people every day. We were able to manage by turning to others to provide a place where they could spend the night after we assisted them."

The U.S. Border Patrol reported nearly 200,000 encounters with migrants along the U.S.-Mexico border in July 2021, the highest monthly total in more than two decades, according to the Pew Research Center.[8] Fiscal year 2021 also had the greatest number of encounters with migrants along the border on record, 1.6 million. The largest numerical increase occurred in the Rio Grande Valley sector, the Pew Center said, adding that the spike was attributed to economic, social, and political instability in some of the migrants' countries of origin.[9] "We managed to survive", Sister Pimentel said. "Aside from 2019, it is the highest numbers we've seen."

Providentially, the circumstances of Sister Pimentel's birth foreshadowed the situation of those who would become her life's work. She was born to Mexican immigrants on July 1, 1953, in Brownsville, Texas, because her father, who hailed from Chiapas, her pregnant mother, originally from Matamoros, and her oldest sister had to wait there while her father's U.S. citizenship application was being processed. "I am a U.S. citizen by '*chiripa*'—sheer chance", she wrote in an essay on immigrants in the book *A Pope Francis*

[8] John Gramlich, "Migrant Encounters at U.S.-Mexico Border Are at a 21-Year High", *Pew Research Center*, August 13, 2021, pewresearch.org/fact-tank/2021/08/13/migrant-encounters-at-u-s-mexico-border-are-at-a-21-year-high/.

[9] John Gramlich and Alissa Scheller, "What's Happening at the U.S.-Mexico Border in 7 Charts", *Pew Research Center*, November 9, 2021, pewresearch.org/fact-tank/2021/11/09/whats-happening-at-the-u-s-mexico-border-in-7-charts/.

Lexicon.[10] Although reared in Brownsville, she wrote that her family often crossed the border to visit relatives and to shop. "I grew up *entre dos fronteras*, enjoying life in two countries, Mexico and the United States."

Before entering religious life at age twenty-four, Sister Pimentel had earned a bachelor of fine arts degree to pursue a promising career as an artist. But she fell in love with Christ, entered her community in 1978, and soon earned a master's in theology.

In the 1980s her community was charged with running Casa Oscar Romero, a shelter for refugees near Brownsville. She ministered there for a decade. In the nineties, after earning a master's degree in counseling, she went to work for Catholic Charities of the Rio Grande Valley in Brownsville, counseling and serving as assistant director. She was named executive director in 2004. Her position includes oversight of emergency assistance, homelessness prevention, disaster relief, clinical counseling, pregnancy care, food programs, and the Humanitarian Resource Center.

"For I was hungry and you gave me food, I was thirsty and you gave me drink, I was a stranger and you welcomed me", Christ says in Matthew 25:35 about the righteous. For her decades doing just that, *Time* magazine included Sister Pimentel on its 2020 list of the hundred most influential people in the world. In 2018 she was awarded the Laetare Medal from Notre Dame University, which recognizes outstanding service to the Church and society. Past recipients include President John F. Kennedy and Catholic Worker founder Dorothy Day. In 2015 she received the Martin Luther King Jr. Keep the Dream Alive award from Catholic Charities for

[10] Sr. Norma Seni Pimentel, "Immigrant", in *A Pope Francis Lexicon*, ed. Joshua J. McElwee and Cindy Wooden (Collegeville, Minn.: Liturgical Press, 2018), 93.

her leadership advancing racial and social justice. She has received numerous other prestigious honors for her work as well. She accepts them in humble gratitude for the spotlight they shine on the plight of those she serves with the help of hundreds of volunteers. "It's an opportunity to bring to light these invisible people who are suffering and hurting—humanity suffering at the border—so the world can see and join in efforts to make sure we do what's right", she said. "They are people, and they have a right to the human dignity and respect a person deserves."

While affirming the importance of keeping the nation's borders safe, Sister Pimentel urges doing so in a humanitarian manner. Her experience at the border has convinced her that it's possible to do both. She works in partnership with U.S. Customs and Border Protection and has witnessed their compassion. She has seen conversion from opposition to her work to support after witnessing it in action. And she experiences the presence of God in the transformations that take place in volunteers and migrants as loving care is given and received.

"My stories of the respite center are of when people show me how important it is to be there for one another", she said. "When we've had hundreds and hundreds and there's almost no space, and someone comes in late at night, the people themselves will make room for each other and say, 'Here, there's room. They'll fit here next to us.' Their response is amazing."

Likewise, she is humbled by the volunteers who come from McAllen and from across the nation to help care for these strangers. "It's amazing how they join in and want to give of their time to be present to the families to hand them milk, a baby bottle, Pampers or a brush or toothpaste", she said. "Those simple things we take for granted mean so much and give hope to someone who's just arriving and has nothing. Those gentle gestures of kindness are a blessing to us all."

She concluded: "Seeing all this, is why when I was asked once what it is we're doing here, I said, 'Restoring human dignity—that's what we're doing.'"

IV
JUSTICE

DEFINING JUSTICE

Justice, like freedom, is invoked not only by murals, poems, and protest placards, but by foundational government documents—worldwide. The United States Constitution famously opens with it ("We the People of the United States, in Order to form a more perfect Union, establish *Justice*, . . . and secure the Blessings of Liberty . . . , do ordain and establish this Constitution"), and even eastern nations such as Iran make it a central pillar ("The Islamic Republic is a system . . . in which equity, justice, political, economic, social, and cultural independence, and national solidarity are secured"). The most radically different of people can agree that justice is a good in itself. But do they have the same idea of justice? How do they define it?

Although some might imagine it to be simply another word for punishment—which is the way the term is used in the North Korean Constitution, for instance—the philosophers of the Western tradition think that justice runs far deeper than this. In fact, it touches every part of life, and it is the key to living well. As Aristotle wrote, "In justice is summed up the *whole of virtue*."[1] Saint Thomas Aquinas shared this broad vision and gave a helpfully short definition: "render[ing] to each one his due." Justice, in other words, is about giving others the good that they deserve, rather than about taking things away. "A man is said to be just," Aquinas says, "because he *respects the rights* of others."[2]

---

[1] See Aristotle, *Ethics*, trans. J.A.K. Thompson, rev. ed. (New York: Penguin, 1976), bk. 5, ch. 1 [1129b30], emphasis added.

[2] Saint Thomas Aquinas, *Summa Theologiae* II-II, q. 58, art. 1, emphasis added.

This respect for rights becomes infinitely richer with the coming of Christ, who is the "sun of justice" (Mal 4:2, Douay-Rheims). Unlike the ancient Greeks, Christians know that the rights (Latin: *jus*) of others come straight from their identity as children of God—as divine royalty, so to speak. Today, some of the most basic human rights that we now take for granted, such as the right to life, proceed from biblical revelation. In pre-Christian Rome, fathers had legal authority to kill their own sons and daughters, a practice called "exposure" so widespread in the ancient world that the second-century Letter of Diognetus found it remarkable Christians "do not expose their infants."[3] Many other foundational rights—such as the right to religious and moral freedom, the right to private property, the right to food and water, the right to healthy working and living conditions, the right to marry freely, the right to be treated as an equal in the eyes of the law, the right to speak out against abusive authorities—all flow from the distinct Christian vision of the human person.[4] Sadly, however, through "blindness and injustice", these rights "are too often disregarded or violated," the *Catechism* observes (*CCC* 1740), and "it is the Church's role to remind men of good will of these rights" (*CCC* 1930). The Catholic heroes you will encounter in this section, Saint Katharine Drexel, Saint Oscar Romero, and Paul and Pat Bokulich, all answered a call to carry out this special work for the Church—a task sometimes called *social justice*.

Among Catholics, social justice is a frequently misunderstood term. It does not begin with law and policy, as many believe, but with personal encounter. Important as law might be, the *Catechism* affirms that "no legislation could

---

[3] "Epistle to Diognetus," in *Early Christian Writings: The Apostolic Fathers*, trans. Maxwell Staniforth (New York: Penguin, 1968), 177, no. 5

[4] See, e.g., Leo XIII, encyclical letter *Rerum Novarum* (May 15, 1891).

by itself do away with the fears, prejudices, and attitudes of pride and selfishness which obstruct the establishment of truly fraternal societies. Such a behavior will cease only through the charity that finds in every man a 'neighbor,' a brother" (*CCC* 1931). Love, not activism, breeds authentic Catholic social justice. Saint Katharine Drexel, heiress of one of the wealthiest families in America, was heartbroken by the unequal opportunities offered to Blacks and Native Americans in the late nineteenth century, so she left behind her own riches to head a religious order that built strong schools for them, including Xavier University in New Orleans, the nation's only historically Black Catholic university. Paul and Pat Bokulich, who fell in love with their Catholic faith at Wayne State University in the early 1960s, understood the Christian-led civil rights movement in the South as a struggle for the *imago Dei*, God's image in man, willing to face tear gas and prison to gain equal voting rights for their Black neighbors.

The Christian faith transfigures social justice. The Marxist revolutions of Central and South America—atheist in nature—show how quickly the quest for rights can slip into untamable violence when God is not heeded. Karl Marx wrote passionately about the rights of man, but viewed God as man's enemy, teaching that "material force must be overthrown by material force."[5] Joseph Ratzinger (Pope Benedict XVI) explains that this attitude, though logical on the surface, runs "contrary to any ethic which is respectful of persons."[6] The battle for justice must be waged instead with courage, dedication, and burning compassion,

[5] Karl Marx, "Critique of Hegel's Philosophy of Right", in *Marx: Early Political Writings*, ed. Joseph O'Malley (Cambridge, U.K.: Cambridge University Press, 1994), 64.

[6] Congregation for the Doctrine of the Faith, Instruction on Certain Aspects of the Theology of Liberation (August 6, 1984).

as Saint Katharine Drexel and Saint Oscar Romero knew. Jesus proclaims, "Blessed are the merciful, for they will be shown mercy. . . . Blessed are the peacemakers, for they shall be called sons of God" (Mt 5:7, 9). This truth forged a two-edged sword for the Bokulich family in the civil rights movement. "Violence was willing to be suffered," Paul remembered, "but not to be given. There are always people who break into violence and hatred. But you can't dispel darkness with darkness. You have to have light to dispel darkness." God alone wins, even when it seems humanly impossible.

CHURCH DOCUMENTS
ON JUSTICE

from U.S. Conference of Catholic Bishops,
Open Wide Our Hearts (2018)

Racism arises when—either consciously or unconsciously—a person holds that his or her own race or ethnicity is superior, and therefore judges persons of other races or ethnicities as inferior and unworthy of equal regard. When this conviction or attitude leads individuals or groups to exclude, ridicule, mistreat, or unjustly discriminate against persons on the basis of their race or ethnicity, it is sinful. Racist acts are sinful because they violate justice. They reveal a failure to acknowledge the human dignity of the persons offended, to recognize them as the neighbors Christ calls us to love (Mt 22:39).

Racism occurs because a person ignores the fundamental truth that, because all humans share a common origin, they are all brothers and sisters, all equally made in the image of God. . . .

Every racist act—every such comment, every joke, every disparaging look as a reaction to the color of skin, ethnicity, or place of origin—is a failure to acknowledge another person as a brother or sister, created in the image of God. . . .

The cumulative effects of personal sins of racism have led to social structures of injustice and violence that makes us all accomplices in racism. . . .

"You have been told, O mortal, what is good, and what the LORD requires of you: Only to do justice and to love goodness, and to walk humbly with your God." (Mic 6:8) To do justice requires an honest acknowledgment of our failures and the restoring of right relationships between us.[1]

from Pope John Paul II, *Centesimus Annus* (1991)

Love for others, and in the first place love for the poor, in whom the Church sees Christ himself, is made concrete in the *promotion of justice*. Justice will never be fully attained unless people see in the poor person, who is asking for help in order to survive, not an annoyance or a burden, but an opportunity for showing kindness and a chance for greater enrichment. Only such an awareness can give the courage needed to face the risk and the change involved in every authentic attempt to come to the aid of another. It is not merely a matter of "giving from one's surplus," but of helping entire peoples which are presently excluded or marginalized to enter into the sphere of economic and human development. For this to happen, it is not enough to draw on the surplus goods which in fact our world abundantly produces; it requires above all a change of life-styles, of models of production and consumption, and of the established structures of power which today govern societies. Nor is it a matter of eliminating instruments of social organization which have proved useful, but rather of orienting them according to an adequate notion of the common good in relation to the whole human family. . . .

Pope Leo XIII's Encyclical [*Rerum Novarum*] also affirms *other rights* as inalienable and proper to the human person.

---

[1] United States Conference of Catholic Bishops, *Open Wide Our Hearts: The Enduring Call to Love* (Washington, D.C.: United States Conference of Catholic Bishops, 2018), usccb.org/resources/open-wide-our-hearts_0.pdf.

Prominent among these . . . is the "natural human right" to form private associations. This means above all *the right to establish professional associations* of employers and workers, or of workers alone. Here we find the reason for the Church's defense and approval of the establishment of what are commonly called trade unions: certainly not because of ideological prejudices or in order to surrender to a class mentality, but because the right of association is a natural right of the human being, which therefore precedes his or her incorporation into political society. . . .

Together with this right, which—it must be stressed— the Pope explicitly acknowledges as belonging to workers, or, using his own language, to "the working class," the Encyclical affirms just as clearly the right to the "limitation of working hours," the right to legitimate rest and the right of children and women to be treated differently with regard to the type and duration of work.

If we keep in mind what history tells us about the practices permitted or at least not excluded by law regarding the way in which workers were employed, without any guarantees as to working hours or the hygienic conditions of the work-place, or even regarding the age and sex of apprentices, we can appreciate the Pope's severe statement: "It is neither just nor human so to grind men down with excessive labor as to stupefy their minds and wear out their bodies." And referring to the "contract" aimed at putting into effect "labor relations" of this sort, he affirms with greater precision, that "in all agreements between employers and workers there is always the condition expressed or understood" that proper rest be allowed, proportionate to "the wear and tear of one's strength." He then concludes: "To agree in any other sense would be against what is right and just."

The Pope immediately adds *another right* which the worker

has as a person. This is the right to a "just wage," which cannot be left to the "free consent of the parties, so that the employer, having paid what was agreed upon, has done his part and seemingly is not called upon to do anything beyond." . . . Every individual has a natural right to procure what is required to live; and the poor can procure that in no other way than by what they can earn through their work.

A workman's wages should be sufficient to enable him to support himself, his wife and his children. If through necessity or fear of a worse evil the workman accepts harder conditions because an employer or contractor will afford no better, he is made the victim of force and injustice.[2]

[2] Pope John Paul II, encyclical letter *Centesimus Annus* (May 1, 1991),vatican.va/content/john-paul-ii/en/encyclicals/documents/hf_jp-ii_enc_0105199 1_centesimus-annus.html.

MOTHER KATHARINE DREXEL

From Heiress to Patron Saint of Racial Justice

In January 1887, wealthy twenty-year-old Katharine Drexel knelt before Pope Leo XIII, and after describing the plight of Native Americans and the few priests ministering to them in the United States, she implored the pontiff to send missionaries to help. To her surprise, he said, "Why do you not become a missionary yourself, my child?"[1]

Katharine, who attended the papal audience with her two sisters, was bewildered. The middle child in a devout, philanthropic Philadelphia family indeed felt called to consecrated life, but to a contemplative order, rather than to an active one. Yet, for some time, Katharine's spiritual director, Bishop James O'Connor, had dissuaded her, urging her instead to continue her charitable work as a laywoman, giving good example to others.

While Katharine keenly desired to help Native Americans with their spiritual and material needs, she also wanted to help African Americans, which was the special interest of her younger sister, Louise. Her elder sister, Elizabeth, favored charities benefitting disadvantaged children.[2] Additionally, all three Drexel sisters gave jointly to many worthy projects.

---

[1] Ellen Tarry, *Katharine Drexel: Friend of the Neglected* (New York: Farrar, Straus & Cudahy, 1958), 158–59.

[2] Lou Baldwin, *A Call to Sanctity: The Formation and Life of Mother Katharine Drexel* (Philadelphia: The Catholic Standard and Times, 1988), 35–36.

The three sisters had recently lost their parents and were very close. Born into one of the wealthiest families in the United States, they were raised to believe their wealth was a gift from God that was meant to be shared with others in need.[3]

Katharine was born on November 26, 1858, in Philadelphia. Her father, Francis Anthony Drexel, was a successful banker as had been his father, Francis Martin Drexel, an immigrant from Austria who had arrived in Philadelphia in 1817 as a portrait artist and later founded the bank Drexel and Co. Katharine was the second child born to Francis and his wife Hannah Langstroth Drexel. Hannah died just five weeks after Katharine's birth. Two years later Francis married Emma Bouvier, who became a beloved stepmother to Katharine and her sister Elizabeth. Katharine and Elizabeth's sister Louise was the daughter of this marriage.

The family were dedicated Catholics. Francis was a well-known philanthropist to a variety of causes who spent a half-hour daily in prayer. Hannah generously distributed material and financial aid to the poor from the family's home three days a week. The Drexel girls helped their mother give alms and taught catechism classes to the children of the employees on their family's summer estate.

Francis Drexel had died suddenly just two years before the Drexel girls' audience with Pope Leo XIII. Their stepmother, Emma, had succumbed to cancer four years prior. The fall after their papal audience, the sisters visited several Native American missions at the invitation of Father Joseph

---

[3] "Saint Katharine Drexel: The Heart of a Woman, the Strength of a Saint", *Sisters of the Blessed Sacrament*, accessed March 20, 2024, katharine drexel.org/katharine-drexel/about-st-katharine-drexel/. See also Cheryl C.D. Hughes, *Katharine Drexel: The Riches-to-Rags Story of an American Catholic Saint* (Grand Rapids, Mich.: Eerdmans Publishing Co., 2014), 19.

Stephan, director of the Catholic Indian Bureau. Bishop O'Connor also accompanied the group. A highlight was befriending famed Sioux Chief Red Cloud at the Pine Bluff Agency in South Dakota. After this trip, Katharine increased her contributions to the missions and reflected on how she could offer further aid.[4]

The next year, on her thirtieth birthday, Katharine wrote to inform Bishop O'Connor that she had resolved to enter religious life: "It appears to me that Our Lord gives me the right to choose the better part, and I shall try to draw as near to his Heart as possible." The bishop relented and suggested three congregations for her consideration. Deeply moved by the poverty and injustices suffered by Native and African Americans, Katharine responded, "I want a missionary order for Indians and Colored people."[5]

Bishop O'Connor suggested she establish such an order, despite her preference for life in a cloister and her concern that she lacked the virtues to guide a congregation as foundress. With the bishop's support and ever aware of Pope Leo XIII's exhortation to become a missionary herself, on March 19, 1889, she discerned that it was God's will for her to found an order to serve Native and African American communities. She desired to give not only her fortune, but her very self. "The feast of St. Joseph brought me the grace to give the remainder of my life to the Indians and Coloreds", she wrote to Bishop O'Connor.

That May, she entered the Sisters of Mercy in Pittsburgh for religious formation. On February 12, 1891, Katharine established the Sisters of the Blessed Sacrament for Indians

---

[4] Cecilia Murray, "Katharine Drexel: Learning to Love the Poor", *Catholic Education: A Journal of Inquiry and Practice* 9, no. 3 (March 2006): 312, files.eric.ed.gov/fulltext/EJ1006058.pdf.

[5] Murray, "Katharine Drexel": 312–13.

and Colored People (known today simply as Sisters of the Blessed Sacrament) when she professed vows as the first religious sister of the order. She took the name Mary Katharine (after the Blessed Mother and Saint Catherine of Siena) and was the first superior general of the order. In addition to the three traditional vows of poverty, chastity, and obedience, she took a fourth vow of service to Native and African Americans.

The next year, she and thirteen companions moved into the newly completed motherhouse in Bensalem, Pennsylvania. They shared the property with a boarding school for Black children they ran. In 1894 they staffed a school for Indian children in Santa Fe, New Mexico. Their work quickly spread to rural and urban areas of the Northeast, the Midwest, the Southwest, and the South.[6]

"At a time when she herself was often living in abject poverty among those to whom she was ministering", writes biographer Ronda De Sola Chervin, "she was dubbed 'the richest nun in the world,' for the fortune she had at her disposal to give away."[7] And give it away she did. The Drexel fortune she inherited as the sole survivor of her family after outliving her sisters amounted to $20 million, which she used to open, staff, and directly support nearly sixty schools and missions, especially in the West and Southwest United States.[8] The most prominent of her educational institutions is the 1925 founding of Xavier University in New Orleans,

[6] "Founding of the Sisters of the Blessed Sacrament", Shrine of Saint Katharine Drexel, accessed November 19, 2023, cathedralphila.org/drexel/learn/founding/.

[7] Ronda De Sola Chervin, *Treasury of Women Saints* (Ann Arbor, Mich.: Servant Publications, 1991), 225.

[8] "Katharine Drexel: 1858–1955", The Holy See, accessed November 10, 2023, vatican.va/news_services/liturgy/saints/ns_lit_doc_20001001_katharine-drexel_en.html.

Louisiana, the first and only historically Black Catholic university in the United States.

At age seventy-seven, while visiting missions in the West, Mother Katharine suffered a severe heart attack. Her declining health forced her into retirement two years later. After she tirelessly led her order for more than four decades, her last eighteen years were spent in prayer, and in this way she unexpectedly realized her initial desire to be a contemplative nun.[9]

Mother Katharine died March 3, 1955, at age ninety-six, at the motherhouse. "Her life had spanned the era of slavery and the Indian wars to the dawn of the modern civil rights movement", notes biographer Robert Ellsberg. "In the era of rigidly enforced racial segregation her work had a profound 'witness value.'"[10]

Mother Katharine was beatified in 1988, just thirty-three years after she died, following the Vatican's confirmation of a miracle credited to her intercession. She was declared a saint on October 1, 2000, after the confirmation of a second miracle. The Vatican named Saint Katharine Drexel patron of racial justice and of philanthropists.

"Her apostolate helped to bring about a growing awareness of the need to combat all forms of racism through education and social services", Pope John Paul II, himself now a canonized saint, said at her canonization Mass. "With great courage and confidence in God's grace, she chose to give not just her fortune but her whole life to the Lord."[11]

[9] John F. Fink, *American Saints: Five Centuries of Heroic Sanctity on the American Continents* (New York: Alba House, 2001), 148.

[10] Robert Ellsberg, *All Saints: Daily Reflections on Saints, Prophets, and Witnesses for Our Time* (Chestnut Ridge, N.Y.: Crossroad Publishing, 1998), 100.

[11] John Paul II, Homily at the Canonization Mass of Katharine Drexel (October 1, 2000), vatican.va/content/john-paul-ii/en/homilies/2000/documents/hf_jp-ii_hom_20001001_canonization.pdf.

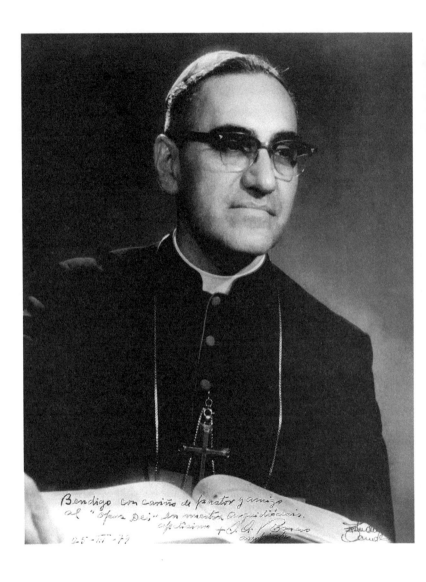

Bendigo con cariño de pastor y amigo
al "Opus Dei" en nuestra Arquidiócesis.
afectísimo + O. A. Romero
arzobispo

25-III-79

SAINT OSCAR ROMERO

The Voice of the Voiceless

It was 1980, a warm Monday evening. Archbishop Oscar Romero of San Salvador, El Salvador, had ended his homily. He was celebrating the Eucharist that day in memory of his friend's mother, in the chapel of the Hospital de la Divina Providencia, where he kept a small apartment. As the archbishop quietly stepped back to the altar to continue Mass, a gunshot shattered the stillness. Pierced through the heart, he collapsed beneath a large crucifix.[1] Romero died within minutes.

A sniper standing in the doorway had silenced this "voice of the voiceless", whose Sunday sermons were eagerly heard by radio listeners all over El Salvador as the only trustworthy source about the human rights atrocities rampant in the country. The archbishop's crime, it seems, had been telling the truth.

Archbishop Romero was sixty-two years old.[2] He had led the archdiocese of San Salvador for three years, seeking justice for his flock. Just minutes before he was shot, he centered his homily on the beauty of the Eucharist—and on the high price of love. "May this Body that is immolated

---

[1] James R. Brockman, *Romero: A Life* (Maryknoll, N.Y.: Orbis Books, 1990), 245. See also "Salvador Archbishop Assassinated by Sniper While Officiating at Mass," *New York Times*, March 25, 1980, nytimes.com/1980/03/25/a rchives/salvador-archbishop-assassinated-by-sniper-while-officiating-at.html.

[2] "Who Was Romero?," *Archbishop Romero Trust*, accessed March 20, 2024, romerotrust.org.uk/who-was-romero.

and this Blood which is sacrificed for men," he proclaimed, "also nourish us so that we can give over our body and our blood to suffering and pain, as Christ did, not for ourselves, but rather so as to bring forth a harvest of justice and peace in our land."[3] The day's Gospel reading had been on the grain of wheat, which is only fruitful if it falls to the earth and dies.

Though he could not know it, these words fittingly described his own untimely death and his own legacy as a courageous champion of justice. For years, Romero had spoken out on behalf of the oppressed poor, denounced the abductions, torture, and murder of community leaders and campesinos—by right-wing militias and left-wing guerrillas alike—and set up programs to help victims of the violence.[4] No one had expected the pious, scholarly Archbishop Romero to become the bold "gospel for El Salvador" he was at the time of his death.[5]

First, he condemned the tyrannical rule of dictator General Carlos Humberto Romero. After the general was removed, he came out even more strongly against the right-wing "junta" that filled the power vacuum and terrorized the country.[6] Unlike many, however, he spoke with spiritual authority, not with political slogans. "Everywhere [in El Salvador], Romero's homilies were people's little morsel for the

[3] Roberto Morozzo Della Rocca, *Oscar Romero: Prophet of Hope* (London: Darton, Longman & Todd, 2015), 216.

[4] "Who Was Romero?" See also Sean-Patrick Lovett, "Remembering St. Oscar Romero: 40 Years after His Assassination," *Vatican News*, March 24, 2020, vaticannews.va/en/church/news/2020-03/oscar-romero-forty-years-assassination-anniversaryo.html.

[5] Robert Ellsberg, *All Saints: Daily Reflections on Saints, Prophets, and Witnesses for Our Time* (New York: Crossroad Publishing, 1997), 132.

[6] *Encyclopaedia Britannica Online*, s.v. "St. Óscar Romero," accessed March 30, 2024, britannica.com/biography/Oscar-Arnulfo-Romero.

day," an accomplice to his murder recalled years later.[7] The broadcast sermons, which catalogued injustices and called for conversion and peaceful change, provided hope to the persecuted, but the powers that be believed they incited the people against them.

Oscar Arnulfo Romero was born on August 15, 1917, in Ciudad Barrios, El Salvador. He was the second of eight children in a family of modest means. At age fourteen, he left a carpentry apprenticeship to enter a local seminary. In 1937, he was sent to Rome where he completed his studies and was ordained a priest on April 4, 1942.

Returning to El Salvador, he lived a simple lifestyle and served more than twenty years in pastoral ministry before being appointed to work in the chancery. In 1970 he was ordained a bishop. Romero chose as his episcopal motto: "Thinking with the Church". He first served as auxiliary bishop of San Salvador and then as bishop of a small rural diocese, Santiago de Maria, before being sent back to the nation's capital to minister as archbishop.

He was installed as archbishop of San Salvador and primate of the Church in El Salvador on February 22, 1977, "amidst unprecedented national tension following fraudulent presidential elections and the massacre of protestors" by military forces.[8]

At the time, an elite group of about fifteen families controlled the nation's politics and economics with the help of military "death squads".[9] Generations of institutionalized social and economic injustice had led to devastating

[7] Carlos Dada, "Así matamos a monseñor Romero", El Faro, March 25, 2010, elfaro.net/es/201003/noticias/1403/.

[8] "The Century of Romero: 1917–2017", Archbishop Romero Trust, accessed March 20, 2024, romerotrust.org.uk/sites/default/files/documents/Century%20of%20Romero%202018%20update.pdf.

[9] Lovett, "Remembering St. Oscar Romero."

disparity. According to Notre Dame University's Kellogg Institute for International Studies:

> Just 2 percent of the population controlled 57 percent of the nation's usable land, and the 16 richest families owned the same amount of land utilized by 230,000 of the poorer families. . . . The poorest families had no land whatever, and were forced to sleep in ditches and muddy fields. . . . Sixty percent of all babies died at birth, and 75 percent of the survivors suffered severe malnutrition. Hundreds of thousands of men, women, and children died from diseases that could have been cured by basic medications.[10]

In response to the violent governmental repression, armed guerrilla groups began to emerge. Soon, anyone sympathetic to the plight of the poor was seen by the military regime as a threat to the status quo. The nation was on the brink of civil war.

Less than three weeks after Archbishop Romero's installation, his good friend Father Rutilio Grande, S.J., an advocate for the poor, was killed by a death squad while driving to a rural town to celebrate Mass. Father Grande's passengers—an elderly male catechist, Manuel Solírzano, and a teenage boy, Nelson Lemus—also died in the ambush. Father Grande was "an example of fidelity unto death," Archbishop Romero told a journalist. "That encouragement and the need to defend a Church that was being persecuted to the point of exterminating the priesthood, impelled me to exercise my pastoral ministry with greater fortitude."[11]

Archbishop Romero became increasingly outspoken in condemning human rights violations, drawing from the

[10] Kellogg Institute for International Studies, "Archbishop Oscar Romero", *Kellogg Institute for International Studies*, University of Notre Dame, accessed March 20, 2024, kellogg.nd.edu/archbishop-oscar-romero.

[11] Patricia Ynestroza, "Saint Oscar Romero: 40th Anniversary of His Murder," produced by Vatican News, March 24, 2020, YouTube video, youtube.com/watch?v=2dYo3-b6Bvc&t=1s.

Gospel and the Church's preferential option for the poor. "The Word of God is like the light of the sun," he said. "It illuminates beautiful things, but also things which we would rather not see."[12] He was nominated for the Nobel Peace Prize in 1979.[13] Vilified by the government-controlled media, he received numerous death threats. When he was offered refuge in Rome, however, he declined. He also refused personal protection, and he traveled about alone so as not to endanger others. "My duty obliges me to walk with my people," he told a journalist about a week before he was murdered. "If death comes, it will be the moment to die as God willed."[14]

The Sunday homily Archbishop Romero preached in the Metropolitan Cathedral the day before his murder signed his death warrant.[15] "Brothers," he appealed to the military, "you are part of our own people. You kill your own campesino brothers and sisters. And before an order to kill that a man may give, God's law must prevail that says, 'Thou shalt not kill!'" Romero did not stop imploring: "No soldier is obliged to obey an order against the law of God. In the name of God, and in the name of this suffering people, whose laments rise to heaven each day more tumultuous. I beg you, I beseech you, I order you in the name of God: Stop the repression!"[16]

This would be his last radio homily. The congregation gave him deafening applause, but to the archbishop's enemies, the words were an act of subversion.[17] The next

[12] Kellogg Institute, "Archbishop Oscar Romero".

[13] *Encyclopaedia Britannica Online*, s.v. "St. Óscar Romero".

[14] Morozzo Della Rocca, *Oscar Romero*, 211.

[15] Kevin Clarke, *Oscar Romero: Love Must Win Out* (Collegeville, Minn.: Liturgical Press, 2014), 24.

[16] Brockman, *Romero: A Life*, 241–42.

[17] Morozzo Della Rocca, *Oscar Romero*, 213.

morning, they learned from the newspaper that Archbishop Romero would celebrate Mass early that evening at the Hospital de la Divina Providencia. Due to the heat, the church doors were left open during the liturgy. A small red car drove up to the church. Through the open door, an assassin fired the shot that claimed the archbishop's life. The car drove off, unapprehended.[18]

Archbishop Romero had become the conscience of El Salvador, a prophet of truth and hope.[19] Not long after his Jeremiah-like voice of justice was silenced, the nation quickly descended into civil war.[20] It would rage for twelve years and claim more than 75,000 lives before ending in 1992.

In 1993, the United Nations' Truth Commission for El Salvador said in its final report that a Salvadoran military officer, "former Major Roberto D'Aubuisson, gave the order to assassinate . . . and gave precise instructions to members of his security detail, which was acting as a 'death squad,' to organize and supervise the assassination."[21] By the time the information came out, it was too late to prosecute D'Aubuisson, who died in 1992. Just days after the UN report was released, the Salvadoran government passed an amnesty law banning the prosecution of war crimes committed during the civil war.

Archbishop Romero was declared a martyr by Pope Francis on February 3, 2015, and was beatified on May 23, 2015, in San Salvador. Francis canonized him just three years later in Rome, on October 14, 2018. Four years later, Father Grande, Solírzano, and Lemus, who had been murdered on

---

[18] Clarke, *Love Must Win Out*, 15, 17.
[19] Morozzo Della Rocca, *Oscar Romero*, 100–101.
[20] Clarke, *Love Must Win Out*, 133–35.
[21] Morozzo Della Rocca, *Oscar Romero*, 218.

their way to celebrate Mass, were also recognized as martyrs and beatified.

"Archbishop Romero," the pope remarked at the canonization, "left the security of the world, even his own safety, in order to give his life according to the Gospel, close to the poor and to his people, with a heart drawn to Jesus and to his brothers and sisters."[22]

As Pope Francis describes it in a letter written for the beatification, the courageous bishop "built peace with the power of love. May those who hold Archbishop Romero as a friend of faith, those who invoke him as protector and intercessor, those who admire his image, find in him the courage to build the Kingdom of God, to commit to a more equal and dignified social order."[23]

[22] Francis, Homily at the Canonization Mass for Oscar Romero (October 14, 2018), vatican.va/content/francesco/en/homilies/2018/documents/papa-francesco_20181014_omelia-canonizzazione.html.
[23] Francis, Letter to the Archbishop of San Salvador for the Beatification of Oscar Romero (May 23, 2015), vatican.va/content/francesco/en/letters/2015/documents/papa-francesco_20150523_lettera-beatificazione-romero.html.

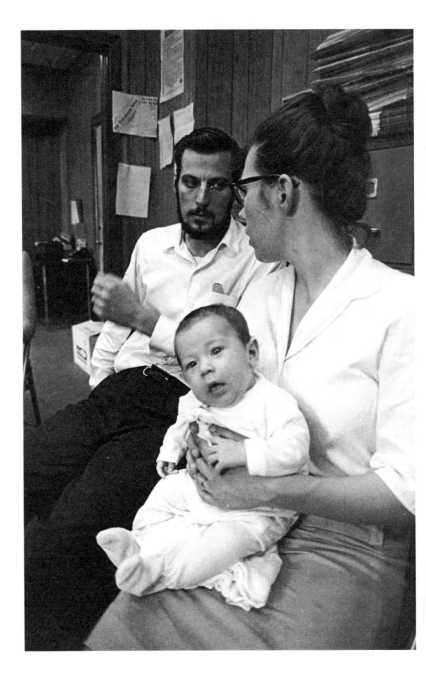

PAUL AND PAT BOKULICH

Living the Gospel Spirit of Selma

It's an iconic image of the civil rights movement. The black-and-white photograph of the 1965 Selma-to-Montgomery March in Alabama shows a stream of peaceful protestors with an American flag cresting a hill while dark thunderclouds loom above them. Their spirited determination to overcome obstacles—the threatening storm and racist policies—to secure voting rights is palpable.[1]

At the center of the photo taken by James Karales during the historic March 21–25 walk, just under the flag representing liberty and justice, a tall white man is tapping the shoulder of a Black girl in front of him. The young man was former seminarian, then-college student Paul Bokulich. He was reminding the girl of rules a federal court had required for the march to take place,[2] which twice before had been brought to an abrupt end: on March 7 in bloodshed when state troopers dispersed the crowd with teargas and clubs, and on March 9 when marchers knelt in prayer before

[1] Linda Merrill, Lisa Rogers, and Kaye Passmore, *Picturing America: Teachers Resource Book*, ed. Carol Peters (Washington, D.C.: National Endowment for the Humanities, 2008), 19b, picturingamerica.neh.gov/downloads/pdfs/Resource_Guide_Chapters/PictAmer_Resource_Book_Chapter_19B.pdf. See also Amy A. Kass and Leon R. Kass, *The Meaning of Martin Luther King Jr. Day: The American Calendar* (Washington, D.C.: What So Proudly We Hail, 2013), 166–67, aei.org/wp-content/uploads/2013/01/-mlk-bookforweb1_16044234 1689.pdf.

[2] Paul Bokulich, telephone interviews with Roxanne King, August 2, 2021 and August 5, 2021.

turning back, postponing the march until a court order providing federal protection was negotiated.[3] "I was reaching over to tell her, 'Little lady, you have to stay in the line. We have to be three abreast'", Bokulich recalled, sharing rules for a stretch alongside a two-lane highway that limited the number of marchers from thousands to just three hundred.[4]

The Detroit native was a twenty-seven-year-old philosophy major at Wayne State University who, with lay and priest friends, answered the call from Reverend Martin Luther King Jr. to join the fifty-four-mile walk after marchers had taken a beating at the Edmund Pettus Bridge in Selma on their first attempt, March 7, which became known as "Bloody Sunday".[5] "I said, 'Yeah! There's nothing here to hold me back'", Bokulich remembered. "I was supposed to be doing incompletes that I wasn't for philosophy. I went along with them."[6]

Now in his eighties, Bokulich didn't even know the famed photo existed until many years later.[7] That is typical for the humble, now-widowed retired gas station/auto-shop owner, who for the last fifty years has lived in Soquel, California.

The march and Reverend King's participation in it aimed to draw attention to racist voting policies that existed and the

[3] Merrill et al., *Picturing America*, 19b. See also Kass and Kass, *Martin Luther King Jr. Day*, 166.

[4] Bokulich, interviews.

[5] Paul Murray, "Selma March at 50: 54-Mile Trek Was 'Magnificent'", *National Catholic Reporter*, March 10, 2015, ncronline.org/blogs/ncr-today/selma-march-50-54-mile-trek-was-magnificent.

[6] Bokulich, interviews.

[7] *You Have to Have Light to Dispel Darkness*, documentary, Sean Schiavolin, director, cinematographer, and editor, 2020, youtube .com/watch?v=wFaLSQ mRNJc&t=37s. See also Isaiah Guzman, "Soquel Man Recalls His Place in Civil Rights Fight: Paul Bokulich Worked under Martin Luther King Jr.", *Santa Cruz Sentinel*, February 29, 2012, santacruzsentinel.com/2012/02/29/so quel-man-recalls-his-place-in-civil-rights-fight-paul-bokulich-worked-under -martin-luther-king-jr/.

need for a national Voting Rights Act. Although thousands walked on the first and last days of the march, Bokulich was among the few hundred who did the entire five-day journey. Because of his experience as an ambulance attendant, he provided first aid and served as a marshal.[8]

Bokulich was a cradle Catholic who attended parochial schools, and his activism was impelled by his faith. Friends who were part of Dorothy Day's Catholic Worker movement in Detroit further sparked his faith, as did strong formation at Wayne State's Catholic Newman Center and the dynamic Paulist priests there. He served as president of the Newman Center and lived in its student housing. "I was taught we are all made *imago dei*—in the image of God— and we should give respect to everybody, which means doing justice to them", Bokulich said. "The Church taught and held up to us love of neighbor. When I went down South, the same thing was preached in the civil rights movement."[9]

Upon his arrival in Selma, Bokulich attended a mass meeting for demonstrators held at Brown Chapel AME Church. Such gatherings taught nonviolence and heartened the activists. "It was an overwhelming experience. It was all spiritual based", he recalled. "They really preached the Lord. Their talks weren't lectures—they were preaching." Stirring Gospel and freedom songs, including the movement's anthem "We Shall Overcome", further bolstered the protestors, as did fervent prayers to endure suffering for the cause. "In the chapel, everyone was there in one spirit", Bokulich said. "The march carried that spirit forward." Bokulich sees the spiritual force of the movement as foundational to its success. He quotes Reverend King:

[8] Murray, "Selma March".
[9] Bokulich, interviews.

"'Unmerited suffering is redemptive'. That was a powerful part of the message."[10]

The nonviolent protests were effective. On March 17, President Lyndon Johnson introduced voting rights legislation to Congress. Four days later, the federally approved civil rights march left Selma protected by National Guardsmen. On March 25, some twenty-five thousand demonstrators victoriously arrived in Montgomery, the capital of Alabama.[11] "It was a joyful celebration", Bokulich said. "The whole impact of a mass of people coming together in one spirit."[12]

On August 6, President Johnson signed the Voting Rights Act of 1965, which prohibits racial discrimination in voting. The U.S. Justice Department calls the act "the single most effective piece of civil rights legislation ever passed by Congress".[13]

After the march, Bokulich briefly returned to Detroit to pack up and move south. "It was the beating at Selma that took me down south", Bokulich said. "It was the spirit of Selma that encouraged me to pack up and return there." He went to Georgia as a staffer for the Southern Christian Leadership Conference, the civil rights organization closely associated with Reverend King. Under the Reverend Hosea Williams, one of King's top leaders, he worked on voter registration drives in Savannah. During that time, he pro-

[10] Ibid. See also *You Have to Have Light*; Catherine Harmon, "A Catholic Looks Back on His Time in the Civil Rights Movement", *Catholic World Report*, January 20, 2020, catholicworldreport.com/2020/01/20/a-catholic-looks-back-on-his-time-in-the-civil-rights-movement/.

[11] "Selma to Montgomery March", *The Martin Luther King Jr. Research and Education Institute, Stanford University*, accessed November 11, 2023, kinginstitute.stanford.edu/encyclopedia/selma-montgomery-march.

[12] Bokulich, interviews.

[13] "The Effect of the Voting Rights Act", *U.S. Department of Justice*, updated August 6, 2015, justice.gov/crt/introduction-federal-voting-rights-laws-0.

posed to Wayne State art student and fellow Detroit native and Catholic activist Pat Grzych Michalak, age twenty-one, who was doing civil rights work in South Carolina.[14]

They married on October 9, 1965, at the Newman Center and started their new life together in Atlanta at the Freedom House, which served as a center for SCLC voter registration drives and a refuge for staffers who needed a place to stay. Inspired by the Gospel, the couple sought a simple lifestyle largely dependent on God's providence. "Friends and relatives put on the wedding for us because we had no money", Bokulich remembers, adding that he was making about $30 a month at SCLC. "We got plain gold wedding bands. As a gift, a friend engraved on them a lily of the field and a bird of the air." The symbols were reminders of Jesus' exhortation to put the kingdom of God and his righteousness first, and as God provides for the lilies of the field and the birds of the air, so too will he provide for such one's needs (Mt 6:25–34). "To a great extent", Bokulich said, "we lived that Scripture."[15]

Pat Bokulich recalled for CRMvet.org, a civil rights movement archive, "We . . . honeymooned for three months at the Freedom House in Atlanta where Paul worked on cars and I learned to cook by feeding at least 20 people each day. Greene County, Eutaw, Alabama, was our next assignment."[16]

The couple lived in a one-and-a-half room shack among sharecroppers in the Black-majority Greene County for three years as they worked on farm co-ops, voter registration drives, and election campaigns. Their first child, a daughter

[14] Bokulich, interviews.
[15] Ibid.
[16] Paul Bokulich and Pat Bokulich, "SCLC, 1965–1968, Alabama, Georgia, South Carolina", first-person account, 2007, *Civil Rights Movement Archive*, accessed November 10, 2023, crmvet.org/vet/bokulich.htm.

born in 1966, was just the second white baby born at Selma's Good Samaritan Hospital, which served the Black community. The hospital, staffed by nuns, had been founded by a Catholic doctor from Germany as an act of reparation after World War II.[17]

Paul Bokulich's activism led to his being jailed numerous times. During the Poor People's Campaign in Washington, D.C., the pregnant Pat and one-year-old Rebecca were teargassed. Once, in Greene County, the Ku Klux Klan left a sign on the Bokulichs' gate urging them to change their ways.[18]

They left Alabama in 1968, before Reverend King's assassination, but their efforts there bore fruit in 1970 when Thomas Gilmore became the first Black sheriff elected in Greene County, after a first try in 1966 that failed because of "voter irregularities".[19] Additionally, a court case, *Paul Bokulich v. the Greene County Jury Commission*, led the U.S. Supreme Court in 1969 to ban "voter suppression-type" laws that prevented Black jurors from serving on grand juries in Alabama.[20]

In 1972 the Bokulichs, who now had two toddlers, moved to Soquel, where their brood ultimately grew to eight children. While Paul ran their business, homemaker Pat did the bookkeeping. She eventually served as director of religious

[17] Bokulich and Bokulich, "SCLC"; Bokulich, interviews. See also *You Have to Have Light*.

[18] Bokulich, interviews. See also Guzman, "Soquel Man" and *You Have to Have Light*.

[19] Bokulich, interviews. See also "Courthouse Square Dedication to Former Sheriff Thomas E. Gilmore Held This Past Saturday", *Washington Informer*, October 22, 2013, washingtoninformer.com/courthouse-square-dedic ation-to-former-sheriff-thomas-e-gilmore-held-this-past-saturday/.

[20] Bokulich, interviews. See also "U.S. Judge Blocks Grand Jury Action", *The Southern Courier*, October 1–2, 1966, crmvet.org/docs /sc/sc661001.pdf; *Bokulich v. Jury Commission*, 394 U.S. 97 (1969).

education at their parish, Saint Joseph's, in nearby Capitola. After retiring, Paul worked maintenance at the parish for many years. Pat died at age sixty-seven in 2012, and Paul still lives in the family home.[21]

"The dignity of the human person has been able to advance because of the way the civil rights movement of that era was conducted", Bokulich reflected. "Violence was willing to be suffered, but not to be given. There are always people who break into violence and hatred. But you can't dispel darkness with darkness. You have to have light to dispel darkness—and love to dispel hatred. It's a great lesson, and the Southern Christian Leadership Conference taught it."[22]

[21] Bokulich, interviews. See also Bokulich and Bokulich, "SCLC" and "Patricia Ann Bokulich", obituary, *Santa Cruz Sentinel*, March 31, 2012, legacy.com/us/obituaries/santacruzsentinel/name/patricia-bokulich-obituary?pid=156775096.
[22] Bokulich, interviews. See also *You Have to Have Light*.

V

CONSCIENCE

DEFINING CONSCIENCE

"The conscience", Pope Pius XII said in 1952, "is the most intimate, most secret core of man."[1] In this quiet sanctuary, deep within, the soul encounters a mysterious voice that guides him in all his decisions—and lets him know if the choice was right, whether he wants to hear it or not. For Saint Paul, "what the law [of God] requires is written on [people's] hearts" (Rom 2:15). This invisible law of the heart is the conscience, and all must answer to it (see Rom 2:16). Nobody escapes conscience. "Even if he would like to," Pope Pius goes on, "[man] could never succeed in shedding it," because it echoes the voice of the Creator.

Conscience, however, often leads us to conclusions that society does not understand. The law "written" on the heart is not always the law of the culture. Before his conversion, Saint Augustine was surrounded by charming, powerful friends living the same wild life he was, yet this camaraderie could not keep him from feeling a "gnaw[ing]" inside.[2] Pope Pius XI writes that in Benito Mussolini's Italy during the 1930s, where Fascism dominated, many Catholic consciences were "tortured by doubts" about joining an influential political party that they knew rejected the Christian faith.[3] In sixteenth-century England, almost all King Henry VIII's Catholic statesmen and bishops signed a

---

[1] Pius XII, Radio Message for the Day of the Family (March 23, 1952) (translated by author).

[2] Saint Augustine, *Confessions*, trans. R.S. Pine-Coffin (New York: Penguin, 1961), bk. 10, chap. 30.

[3] Pius XI, encyclical letter *Noi Abbiamo Bisogno* (June 29, 1931), nos. 58–59.

declaration calling the king the true head of the Church—
a small, painless, and politically advantageous gesture that
Saint Thomas More's conscience called him to refuse.
"Deep within," posits the *Catechism*, "man discovers a law
which he has not laid upon himself but which he must
obey" (*CCC* 1776, citing *Gaudium et Spes*, no. 16). It is
infinitely higher than any state legislation, and it sometimes
proves costly. More's loyalty to his conscience landed him
a death sentence for the gravest crime in the land: treason.

Yet the conscience needs training. "The education of the
conscience is a lifelong task," the *Catechism* affirms (*CCC*
1784). Servant of God Dorothy Day had been an activist
for workers' rights since her youth, but only after a long
conversion from anarchism to Catholicism did her con-
victions about human dignity finally take root, allowing
her to focus her work. Blessed Franz Jägerstätter spent his
early years drinking, fighting, and riding motorcycles in
his Austrian village, but when he eventually dove into in
the teachings of Christ, he found himself compelled to
resist the Nazi Third Reich at the cost of his life. Servant
of God Sister Thea Bowman, who grew up in a working-
class Black family in segregated Mississippi, received her
education from Franciscan nuns, who gave her not only
an unshakeable sense of her own beauty and dignity, but
a sharp conscience that commanded her to spend her life
helping the Church to reach out to Black Catholics like
herself, spreading the fire of joy.

Man's conscience is both sacred and "secret" (*CCC*
1776). Although it is dependent on time, place, and concrete circumstances, it is also free.[4] Since each person is
made in the image and likeness of the eternal God, each

[4] See Pius XI, *Noi Abbiamo Bisogno*; Leo XIII, encyclical letter *Libertas*
(June 20, 1888); *CCC* 1778–1880.

person is a mystery, and nobody quite knows the designs that God has for someone else's life—or even for one's own life. Nobody could have predicted the Shakespearean drama that would gradually unfold through the missions of Dorothy Day, Franz Jägerstätter, and Sister Thea Bowman, all three of them ordinary people with ordinary beginnings, whose consciences spurred them to quiet heroism. Yet by listening each day for the voice of God, learning from the ancient wisdom of the Church, and generously following our conscience, we too can see our lives shape into a heroic masterpiece—a complex and luminous mosaic, built of a million tiny, everyday choices.

CHURCH DOCUMENTS
ON CONSCIENCE

from U.S. Bishops, "Discrimination and Christian Conscience" (1958)

Our Christian faith is of its nature universal. It knows not the distinctions of race, color, or nationhood. . . . Even those who do not accept our Christian tradition should at least acknowledge that God has implanted in the souls of all men some knowledge of the natural moral law and a respect for its teachings. Reason alone taught philosophers through the ages respect for the sacred dignity of each human being and the fundamental rights of man. Every man has an equal right to life, to justice before the law, to marry and rear a family under humane conditions, and to an equitable opportunity to use the goods of this earth for his needs and those of his family.[1]

from Pope John XXIII, encyclical letter *Pacem in Terris* (1963)

The world's Creator has stamped man's inmost being with an order revealed to man by his conscience; and his conscience insists on his preserving it. Men "show the work

[1] Catholic Bishops of the United States, "Discrimination and Christian Conscience (November 14, 1958)", in *Pastoral Letters of the United States Catholic Bishops*, vol. 2 (Washington, D.C.: United States Catholic Conference, 1990), usccb.org/issues-and-action/cultural-diversity/african-american/resou rces/upload/Discrimination-Christian-Conscience-Nov-14-1958.pdf.

of the law written in their hearts. Their conscience bears witness to them." And how could it be otherwise? All created being reflects the infinite wisdom of God. It reflects it all the more clearly, the higher it stands in the scale of perfection.[2]

from Pontifical Council for Justice and Peace, *The Church and Racism* (1988)

Respect for every person and every race is respect for basic rights, dignity and fundamental equality. This does not mean erasing cultural differences. Instead it is important to educate to a positive appreciation of the complementary diversity of peoples. A well-understood pluralism resolves the problem of closed racism. . . .

The Church wants first and foremost to change racist attitudes, including those within her own communities. . . . Her mission is to give soul to this immense undertaking of human fraternity. Despite the sinful limitations of her members, yesterday and today, she is aware of having been constituted a witness to Christ's charity on earth, a sign and instrument of the unity of humankind. The message she proposes to everyone, and which she tries to live is: "Every person is my brother or sister."[3]

---

[2] John XXIII, encyclical letter *Pacem in Terris* (April 11, 1963), vatican.va /content/john-xxiii/en/encyclicals/documents/hf_j-xxiii_enc_11041963_pace m.html.

[3] Pontifical Council for Justice and Peace, *The Church and Racism: Towards a More Fraternal Society* (August 31, 2001), humandevelopment.va/content/dam /sviluppoumano/pubblicazioni-documenti/archivio/diritti-umani/The%20C hurch%20against%20Racism%202001-1988.pdf.

from Pope John Paul II, *Veritatis Splendor* (1993)

The relationship between man's freedom and God's law is most deeply lived out in the "heart" of the person, in his moral conscience. As the Second Vatican Council observed [in *Gaudium et Spes*]: "In the depths of his conscience man detects a law which he does not impose on himself, but which holds him to obedience. Always summoning him to love good and avoid evil, the voice of conscience can when necessary speak to his heart more specifically: *do this, shun that.* For man has in his heart a law written by God. To obey it is the very dignity of man; according to it he will be judged (cf. Rom 2:14–16)." . . .

The voice of conscience has always clearly recalled that there are truths and moral values for which one must be prepared to give up one's life. In an individual's words and above all in the sacrifice of his life for a moral value, the Church sees a single testimony to that truth which, already present in creation, shines forth in its fullness on the face of Christ.[4]

[4] John Paul II, encyclical letter *Veritatis Splendor* (August 6, 1993), vatic an.va/content/john-paul-ii/en/encyclicals/documents/hf_jp-ii_enc_06081993 _veritatis-splendor.html.

14

DOROTHY DAY

A Woman of Conscience

When Pope Francis addressed a joint meeting of Congress in Washington, D.C., on September 24, 2015, becoming the first pontiff to do so, he included journalist and social activist Dorothy Day among four "great" Americans—along with Abraham Lincoln, Martin Luther King Jr., and Thomas Merton—who he said represent the values and spirit of the American people.[1] About Day, Catholic convert and co-founder of the *Catholic Worker* newspaper and movement, he said, "Her social activism, her passion for justice, and for the cause of the oppressed, were inspired by the Gospel, her faith, and the example of the saints."[2]

Pope Francis held up Day, who in the Church has the title Servant of God, as a model for the passion we should have in working to protect the rights of persons. He said, "A nation can be considered great . . . when it strives for justice and the cause of the oppressed, as Dorothy Day did by her tireless work."[3] For those efforts, the Dorothy Day Guild, which exists to promote the cause for her canonization that opened February 2002, calls her "a woman of conscience".[4]

[1] Francis, Visit to the Joint Session of the United States Congress (Washington, D.C.: September 24, 2015), vatican.va/content/francesco/en/speeches/2015/september/documents/papa-francesco_20150924_usa-us-congress.html.

[2] Francis, U.S. Congress.

[3] Ibid.

[4] Carolyn Zablotny, "A Woman of Conscience", Dorothy Day Guild, accessed March 20, 2024, dorothydayguild.org/a-woman-of-conscience.

Although her road to faith was winding, she may one day officially be called a saint.

Born on November 8, 1897, in Brooklyn, New York, Dorothy was one of the five children of homemaker Grace and sportswriter John Day. The family moved to Oakland, California, when Dorothy was six years old. The devastation and loss caused by the 1906 San Francisco earthquake left her with vivid memories. Her father lost his job and her mother helped those left homeless. The family was forced to relocate to Chicago, where Dorothy recalled a childhood that included a brief time of hardship followed by middle-class comfort.[5]

Although Protestant, the family rarely attended church. Even so, Dorothy experienced times of piety inspired by Bible reading and the witness of devout neighbors. At age eight she attended Sunday school and church with Methodist neighbors. In Chicago, she began to pray regularly after coming upon a Catholic friend's mother kneeling in prayer. Later, she began attending the Episcopal church where her brothers sang in the choir. At age thirteen, after studying the catechism, she was baptized and confirmed in the Episcopal church.[6]

At fifteen, she encountered anarchism and socialism in her reading, a favorite pastime. She was especially moved by Upton Sinclair's exposé of the meatpacking industry, *The Jungle*, in which the protagonist finds promise in socialism. Her conscience roused, she began exploring poor neighbor-

[5] James Allaire and Rosemary Broughton, "An Introduction to the Life and Spirituality of Dorothy Day", excerpt from *Praying with Dorothy Day: Companions for the Journey* (Winona, Minn.: St. Mary's Press, 1995), *Catholic Worker Movement*, accessed March 25, 2024, catholicworker.org/life-and-spirituality-dorothy-day/.

[6] Allaire and Broughton, "Introduction".

hoods.[7] "The very fact that *The Jungle* was about Chicago where I lived, whose streets I walked, made me feel that from then on my life was to be linked to theirs, their interests were to be mine," Dorothy recalled in her autobiography, *The Long Loneliness*. "I had received a call, a vocation, a direction to my life."[8]

She graduated from high school at sixteen and began attending the University of Illinois on a scholarship. Feeling that Christians working to address injustice were few, and stirred by the Marxist slogan "Workers of the world unite! You have nothing to lose but your chains", she joined the Socialist party. She did domestic work to support herself and indulged her love of writing by penning articles for a local newspaper. Her faith became increasingly fragile, although the works of Dostoevsky and Tolstoy helped her hold on to it for a while.[9] But when a professor suggested that the strong do not need religion, "I felt that I must turn from it as from a drug", she recalled. Keenly aware that relief aid treated symptoms but not the cause of social ills, she wondered where the saints were who would "try to change the social order, not just to minister to the slaves but to do away with slavery".[10]

She left college after two years and sought work as a journalist in New York. There she labored for socialist publications by day and caroused with radicals and celebrated writers and artists at night. In 1917 she was jailed for demonstrating outside the White House to protest the treatment

---

[7] Dorothy Day, *The Long Loneliness: An Autobiography* (New York: Harper & Row, 1952), 36–38. See also Jim Forest, *All Is Grace: A Biography of Dorothy Day* (Maryknoll, N.Y.: Orbis Books, 2011), 18–19.

[8] Day, *Long Loneliness*, 38.

[9] Ibid., 39–43.

[10] Ibid., 43, 45.

of incarcerated women suffragists. While imprisoned, she participated in a successful hunger strike to be recognized as a political prisoner. The following year, with the United States involved in World War I and the 1918 flu epidemic raging, Dorothy, wanting to help directly, worked as a nurse in training for a time in Brooklyn.[11]

Over the next few years, Dorothy experienced a love affair that tragically ended with an abortion in a failed attempt to save the relationship, a brief rebound marriage, and an attempted suicide. She recounted some of these experiences in the autobiographical novel *The Eleventh Virgin*. With the money she got for the book's screen rights, she bought a beach house in Staten Island. While living there and working as a freelancer, she lived in a common-law marriage with biologist Forster Batterham, who was atheist and anarchist.[12]

Dorothy referred to this period of delighting in nature and intense love as a time of "natural happiness" that brought her to God. The high point of her joy was learning she was pregnant, as she had longed for a child but had believed the abortion had made her sterile.[13]

Forster, however, did not share her happiness. He was adamantly opposed to both marriage and children. When her daughter, Tamar, was born on March 4, 1926, Dorothy, who had found herself praying and attending Mass, had already made a life-changing decision. "I knew that I was going to have my child baptized, cost what it may", she recalled. "I felt it was the greatest thing I could do for my child."[14]

Dorothy prayed for the gift of faith and waited for the

---

[11] Forest, *All Is Grace*, 24–27, 36, 39–41, 44, 48.

[12] Ibid., 51–58, 65–67.

[13] Day, *Long Loneliness*, 134–36.

[14] Ibid., 136.

right moment. "It got to the point", she wrote, "where it was the simple question of whether I chose God or man." She chose God and settled on the Catholic Church, believing it to be "the Church of the poor". Dorothy had Tamar baptized in July 1927. That December she ended her common-law relationship with Forster and was baptized herself.[15]

For the next five years she sought a way to tie her faith with her work and passion for social justice.[16] The opportunity arose in 1932 when she covered the December 8 Hunger March in Washington, D.C., for Catholic magazines as a freelancer. The Communist-organized protest aimed to draw attention to the plight of the unemployed experiencing the third year of the Great Depression.[17]

Dorothy took pride in the courage of the marchers—the vast majority of whom were not Communist, she reported—but was disappointed that her own contribution to their cause was limited to writing about it.[18] After the event was over and her story was written, on the feast of the Immaculate Conception—a holy day honoring Mary—Dorothy visited the crypt church beneath the National Shrine of the Immaculate Conception, which was then under construction. "There I offered up a special prayer, a prayer which came with tears and with anguish, that some way would open up for me to use what talents I possessed for my fellow workers, for the poor", she recalled. "And when I returned to New York, I found Peter Maurin."[19]

Peter, a French immigrant, was a former Christian Brothers teacher who had a vision for society based on Gospel

[15] Ibid., 136, 140, 143, 148, 150.
[16] Forest, *All Is Grace*, 87.
[17] Ibid., 96–99. See also Allaire and Broughton, "Introduction".
[18] Ibid., 99. See also Allaire and Broughton, "Introduction."
[19] Day, *Long Loneliness*, 166.

values and Catholic social teaching. An editor had referred him to Dorothy. He was waiting for her when she arrived home the day after the Hunger March. She quickly saw Peter as the answer to her prayers. Likewise, Peter saw Dorothy as the collaborator he had prayed for.[20] Together, trusting in providence to pay the bills, they started the *Catholic Worker* newspaper to promote Catholic social teaching and to "arouse the conscience" of the reader, as Dorothy wrote in the May 1977 issue of the *Catholic Worker*. They sold the first issue at Union Square on May 1, 1933, for a penny a copy.[21]

Peter's threefold "new social order" was based on founding a newspaper to help people think according to Gospel values, promoting houses of hospitality to feed the hungry and shelter the homeless, and establishing farming communes to enable people to "return to the land". The *Catholic Worker* promoted those ideas via Peter's "Easy Essays", while Dorothy reported on homelessness and unemployment.[22] Soon, readers came looking for resources, while others were inspired to help provide them, and the Catholic Worker Movement was born. Eventually, the movement also embraced voluntary poverty and pacifism.[23]

Peter died at the Catholic Worker's Maryfarm near Newburgh, New York, on May 15, 1949. Dorothy continued serving the poor and the oppressed through the *Catholic*

[20] Forest, *All Is Grace*, 108. See also Jim Forest, "Biography of Peter Maurin", *Catholic Worker Movement*, February 11, 2022, catholicworker.org/peter maurin/pm-biography.html.

[21] Dorothy Day, "Peter Maurin, 1877–1977", *The Catholic Worker*, May 1, 1977, thecatholicnewsarchive.org/?a=d&d=CW19770501-01.2.3&e=------- en-20--1--txt-txIN--------. See also Forest, "Biography of Peter Maurin" and Allaire and Broughton, "Introduction".

[22] Forest, *All Is Grace*, 101–2.

[23] Allaire and Broughton, "Introduction".

Worker newspaper and movement until her own death thirty-one years later. Following her "astute social conscience", she was jailed seven times over the decades for acts of nonviolent civil disobedience.[24] She was arrested for the first time at age twenty, when she picketed for women's suffrage in 1917, and for the last time at age seventy-five for protesting with Cesar Chavez's striking farm laborers in 1973.[25] Dorothy died at the Catholic Worker's Maryhouse in New York City on November 29, 1980.

Today, the *Catholic Worker* newspaper is still available for a penny a copy. Nearly two hundred Catholic Worker houses of hospitality now exist around the world and more than twenty Catholic Worker farms dot the globe, with the vast majority in the United States.[26]

At the time of Dorothy's death, many saw her as "the heart and conscience of the American Church".[27] Her cause for canonization was opened in the year 2000 and she was given the title Servant of God. She lived the Gospel message radically and often quoted novelist Leon Bloy: "There is only one sadness: not to be a saint."[28]

[24] Zablotny, "A Woman of Conscience".

[25] "Thirty Interesting Facts about Dorothy Day's Life", Catholic Worker Movement, February 11, 2022, catholicworker.org/dorothyday/dd-interesting-facts.html.

[26] "Directory of Catholic Worker Communities", Catholic Worker Movement, accessed November 13, 2022, catholicworker.org/communities/directory-picker.html.

[27] Carolyn Zablotny, "Movement to Canonize Dorothy Day", *Dorothy Day Guild*, 2023, dorothydayguild.org/timeline/movement-to-canonize -dorothy-day.

[28] Zablotny, "Movement to Canonize Dorothy Day".

BLESSED FRANZ JÄGERSTÄTTER

A Solitary Witness

Franz Jägerstätter loved his wife deeply, adored his daughters, and relished the beauty of nature that surrounded his farm in the Austrian village of St. Radegund. A devout Catholic, he volunteered as church sexton arranging liturgies, perhaps to thank God who had so richly blessed him with domestic happiness after a challenging childhood and somewhat rowdy youth.

Despite his near-perfect bliss, Franz was impelled by his conscience to calmly walk to the guillotine in Berlin-Brandenburg prison at 4:00 P.M. on August 9, 1943. He was swiftly beheaded by German military as an "enemy of the state" for refusing to swear allegiance to Adolf Hitler and fight what he asserted was an "unjust war".[1] He was thirty-six years old.

Franz had been drafted into active duty just six months earlier. Family members, friends, his pastor, and his bishop had all counseled Franz to obey the Third Reich to save himself, and for the sake of his family. But Franz remained undeterred.

"To take the military oath would be nothing other than collaboration with evil, since it would require of him an affirmation of loyalty to the Fuhrer that he rejected with all

---

[1] Thomas Merton, *Faith and Violence: Christian Teaching and Christian Practice* (Notre Dame, Ind.: University of Notre Dame Press, 1968), 69.

his soul", writes Brian Wicker. "Such a lie was something he would not tell even to protect himself and his loved ones. It is also why today he is accepted as a genuine martyr."[2]

Franz was born in St. Radegund on May 20, 1907, to maidservant Rosalia Huber and farmer's son Franz Bachmeier (who later died in the First World War). The couple did not marry, and Franz was initially cared for by his pious widowed grandmother, Elisabeth Huber. He went to school for just eight years, mostly attending a one-room schoolhouse. When Franz was ten, his mother married Heinrich Jägerstätter, a farmer, who adopted him.

As a young man, Franz worked for three years in mining in another town. When he returned to St. Radegund, he was the first person in the village to own a motorcycle. In 1933, he fathered a child out of wedlock. The following year, he was arrested with fellow members of a gang for fighting.

In his late twenties, Franz began to take his faith seriously. At one point, he considered entering a monastery.[3] In 1936, on Holy Thursday, he married Franziska Schwaninger, a fervent Catholic. For their honeymoon, they went on pilgrimage to Rome and received a papal blessing.

"We helped one another go forward in faith", Franziska once observed, recalling their spiritual life.[4] They prayed together, and Franz enjoyed reading the lives of the saints. The Bible became their guide for everyday life. Within four years, their family had grown to include three daughters. (Franz also visited and helped support the daughter he had

[2] Brian Wicker, "The Significance of Franz Jägerstätter", *New Blackfriars* 89, no. 1022 (July 2008): 388.

[3] Jim Forest, "Introduction", in *Franz Jägerstätter: Letters and Writings from Prison*, ed. Erna Putz (Maryknoll, N.Y.: Orbis Books, 2009), xiv.

[4] Forest, "Introduction", xv.

fathered before his marriage.) Filled with awe, Franz once told Franziska, "I never could have imagined that being married could be so wonderful."[5]

In March 1938, German troops invaded Austria and annexed it to the Third Reich. In April, the annexation (called the *Anschluss*) was ratified by popular ballot. Franz was the only person in his village to vote against the annexation. But to prevent endangering the village, city officials claimed the vote was unanimous. Villagers were well aware Franz saw the annexation as akin to the crowd in Jerusalem choosing the murderer Barabbas over the savior, Jesus. When met with the Nazi salute and greeting "Heil Hitler", Franz would respond "Pfui [phooey] Hitler" without saluting.[6]

Franz had had a dream that strengthened his anti-Nazi conviction. He saw "a beautiful shining railroad train" circling a mountain. "Streams of children—and adults as well—rushed toward the train." Then he heard a voice say, "This train is going to hell."[7] He realized the train represented the Nazi regime and its organizations, primarily the Hitler Youth.

"The dream seemed to Franz a clarifying message from heaven", writes biographer Jim Forest. "The Nazi movement—with its racism, its cult of violence, its elimination of those members of society regarded as unfit, its efforts to suppress Christianity—was satanic. It was nothing less than a gateway to hell."[8]

---

[5] "Franz Jägerstätter 1907–1943, Martyr, Short Biography", *Linz Diocese*, accessed November 14, 2023, dioezese-linz.at/site/jaegerstaetter/english/biography/article/22528.html.

[6] Forest, "Introduction", xvii.

[7] Gordon Zahn, *In Solitary Witness: The Life and Death of Franz Jägerstätter* (New York: Beacon Press, 1964), 111.

[8] Forest, "Introduction", xvii.

In June 1940, Franz was drafted into the German army and received military training. He received a deferment after a few months before again being called up in the fall for further training. That year, Franz began serving as a sexton at his church and he became a Third Order Franciscan, a group whose members follow the Franciscan rule of life as laypeople. In April 1941 he got another deferment as a working farmer.[9]

On February 23, 1943, Franz was called up for combat duty. He arrived at the induction center in Enns, Austria, on March 1. He refused to take the military oath, explaining that he would not fight but that he would serve as a paramedic. His offer was denied.[10]

Franz was arrested and imprisoned in Linz, Austria, for two months before being imprisoned in Berlin-Tegel, Germany, in May, where he was tried on July 6, 1943. He was condemned to death for sedition, and the sentence was confirmed on July 14. He was transferred to Berlin-Brandenburg prison for execution. "If I must write . . . with my hands in chains, I find that much better than if my will were in chains", Franz wrote in prison shortly before his execution. "Neither prison nor chains nor sentence of death can rob a man of the faith and his free will. God gives so much strength that it is possible to bear any suffering. . . . People worry about the obligations of conscience as they concern my wife and children. But I cannot believe that, just because one has a wife and children, a man is free to offend God."[11]

[9] Samuel Warde, "Franz Jägerstätter Chose the Guillotine over Pledging Loyalty to Hitler", *All That's Interesting*, updated January 2, 2020, allthatsinteresting.com/franz-jagerstatter.

[10] "Bl. Franz Jägerstätter (1907–1943): Layman and Martyr", *The Holy See*, accessed November 14, 2023, vatican.va/news_services/liturgy/saints/ns_lit_doc_20071026_jagerstatter_en.html.

[11] "Bl. Franz Jägerstätter".

On the eve of Franz's execution, prison chaplain Father Albert Jochmann told Franz that if he signed a form consenting to military service, his life would be spared. Franz refused, and his serene resoluteness struck the priest. The next day, he spent time ministering to Franz prior to his beheading. He later said, "I say with certainty that this simple man is the only saint that I have ever met in my lifetime."[12]

On May 7, 1997, the District Court of Berlin officially annulled Franz's original death sentence, "in effect acquitting him because of the moral and legal justification of his actions".[13]

On June 1, 2007, the Vatican declared that Franz was a martyr. Four months later, on October 26, 2007, Franz was declared Blessed. His widow, Franziska, then age ninety-four, the couple's three daughters, and the daughter Franz had fathered prior to his marriage were in attendance at his beatification in Linz, Austria.

"Franz Jägerstätter is a prophet with a global view and a penetrating insight which very few of his contemporaries had at that time", Linz Bishop Ludwig Schwarz said in a statement at the time of the beatification. "He is a shining example in his fidelity to the claims of his conscience."[14]

---

[12] Daniel Hallock, "Franz Jägerstätter, A Quiet Martyr", *Plough*, May 28, 2019, plough.com/en/topics/justice/nonviolence/franz-jagerstatter-a-quiet-martyr.

[13] Michael Miller, "Previously Unknown Document by Blessed Franz Jägerstätter Discovered", *Catholic World Report*, June 5, 2022, catholicworld report.com/2022/06/05/previously-unknown-document-by-blessed-franz-ja gerstatter-discovered/.

[14] "Franz Jägerstätter 1907–1943, Martyr".

16

SISTER THEA BOWMAN

"True Truth"—Testifying Evangelist

When Sister Thea Bowman addressed the United States
Catholic bishops on June 17, 1989, she had long been what
she called a "fully functioning" Black Catholic—so much
so that the Franciscan Sister of Perpetual Adoration was
able to speak the truth her conscience urged to the bishops
with heartfelt love. Her remarks on what it means to be
Black in the Catholic Church challenged, convicted, and
inspired them. "I bring myself; my black self, all that I am,
all that I have, all that I hope to become", she said, defin-
ing "fully functioning". "I bring my whole history, my tra-
ditions, my experience, my culture, my African-American
song and dance and gesture and movement and teaching and
preaching and healing and responsibility—as gifts to the
Church."[1]

She was an evangelist, singing and preaching the "true
truth"—saying what needed to be said—to the U.S. Church
hierarchy at their spring meeting. Seated in a wheelchair, her
body riddled with cancer, she made her profound observa-
tions with urgency. In a colorful African dress, often flashing

[1] Thea Bowman, "Sr. Thea Bowman's Address to the United States
Bishop's Conference, June 1989", usccb.org/issues-and-action/cultural-diver
sity/african-american/resources/upload/Transcript-Sr-Thea-Bowman-June-1
989-Address.pdf.

her bright smile, exuding joy, she was the spirituals-singing, whole-truth testifying "conscience of the Church".[2]

Describing that gathering held at Seton Hall University in East Orange, New Jersey, biographer Maurice J. Nutt writes: "Even in her sickness and fragility [she] delivered an unforgettable, well-crafted, and—in her typical Thea folksy fashion—spontaneous message on the struggle for racial justice and the need for evangelization, Catholic education, and full participation and inclusivity for black Catholics in the Roman Catholic Church in America. In a word, Thea was masterful."[3]

The charismatic sister, who was an educator, scholar, vocalist, intercultural awareness advocate, and the great-granddaughter of former slaves,[4] was such a popular evangelist that she had been featured on the television news magazine 60 Minutes two years prior. On the day of her meeting with the bishops, they were visibly moved, some shedding tears, at her powerfully delivered message. At the end, she got them to cross their arms and hold hands with one another while singing the hymn that had become the civil rights anthem, "We Shall Overcome". Nine months later, on March 30, 1990, Sister Thea died. She was fifty-two.

She was given the name Bertha Elizabeth Bowman when she was born on December 29, 1937, in Yazoo City, Mississippi. Her parents, Theon and Mary Esther Coleman

[2] Richard Szczepanowski, "Catholic University Names Street in Honor of Sister Thea Bowman", *Catholic News Service*, May 2, 2022, catholicnews.com/catholic-university-names-street-in-honor-of-sister-thea-bowman/.

[3] Maurice J. Nutt, C.Ss.R., *Thea Bowman: Faithful and Free* (Collegeville, Minn.: Liturgical Press, 2019), 7.

[4] Charlene Smith and John Feister, *Thea's Song: The Life of Thea Bowman* (Maryknoll, N.Y.: Orbis Books, 2009), Kindle.

Bowman, gave their only child a middle-class upbringing in nearby Canton, Mississippi. Theon was a doctor and Mary Esther was a teacher. Sister Thea often referred to herself as an "old folks'" child because her parents were middle-aged when she was born.

Despite being well loved and intelligent, while in grade school, due to the inferior education given in underfunded Black schools in the then-segregated South, Bertha was behind in reading. When Catholic priests and nuns opened a mission school for Black children in Canton, the Bowmans enrolled their daughter in Holy Child Jesus School's first sixth-grade class in 1948.

Bertha, whose family worshiped at the Episcopalian and Methodist churches, had been so impressed by the outreach of the Catholic religious men and women to the Black community that she had converted to Catholicism the previous year at age nine. The school was staffed by Franciscan Sisters of Perpetual Adoration. She adored the nuns, about whom she later said, "We loved our teachers, because they first loved us."[5]

At age fifteen, Bertha told her parents she wanted to enter the FSPA order. When they said no—they did not convert to Catholicism until years later—she went on a hunger strike, which soon won their permission. She became the first African American nun of the Franciscan Sisters of Perpetual Adoration, entering formation in 1953 at the motherhouse in LaCrosse, Wisconsin.

A nun from the order, Sister Lina Putz, accompanied Bertha on the train trip from Mississippi to Wisconsin. Although Jim Crow law was in force, remarkably, the Franciscan

___

[5] Ibid.

Sisters got permission for Bertha to travel with Sister Lina in a "whites only" passenger car for the journey. The *LaCrosse Catholic Register* ran a story about Bertha's historic entry into the all-white religious order under the headline "Negro Aspirant".[6]

Three years into formation, Bertha took the religious name Thea, which means "of God" and is a feminine version of her father's name, Theon.[7] She had graduated from her congregation's Saint Rose High School despite a year-long bout with tuberculosis that required a stay in a sanatorium.

She next pursued studies at Viterbo College (now Viterbo University) in LaCrosse, also run by her congregation. Trained as a teacher, she earned a bachelor's degree in English, speech, and drama. She later attended the Catholic University of America in Washington, D.C., where she earned master's and doctoral degrees in English, literature, and linguistics.

Both her master's thesis and doctoral dissertation focused on the rhetorical skills of the martyr of moral conscience statesman Saint Thomas More. Although a former favorite of Henry VIII, More was executed in 1535 for refusing to recognize Henry as supreme head of the Church in England. The king desired that power because of the Catholic pope's refusal to annul his marriage to Catherine of Aragon. More's famous last words speak to his refusal to betray his conscience: "I die the king's good servant, but God's first." For her doctoral dissertation, Sister Thea analyzed a book More wrote while imprisoned the last year of his life, *A Di-*

[6] Ibid.
[7] Ibid.

alogue of Comfort against Tribulation. In it, "More logically—
and sometimes humorously—explained the power of choosing right even if it meant grief for oneself and loved ones."[8]

Sister Thea's biographers Charlene Smith and John Feister
noted: "Everything about More's spirit came alive for Thea.
His intellectualism, his humor, his discipline, his devotion
to family, his attitude toward suffering, his defense of truth
were characteristics she emulated. He had become one of
her heroes. . . . Thea likewise was elated with the rhetoric
More used. . . . She incorporated Morian techniques of ex-
position, logic and persuasion into her own subsequent writing, teaching, and speaking."[9]

As an educator for more than fifteen years, Sister Thea
taught youth at Blessed Sacrament School in LaCrosse and
at Holy Child Jesus High School in Canton, before serving
as a professor at Viterbo College, the Catholic University
of America (CUA), and Xavier University in Louisiana. At
Xavier, she helped establish the Institute for Black Catholic
Studies in 1980.

But her wide-ranging ministry was full of accomplish-
ments, many of which flowed from her mission to re-inspire
the Black community with Christ's message. In 1968, while
attending CUA, Sister Thea became a founding member
of the National Black Sisters Conference, where her public speaking and singing began in earnest. In 1978, she returned to Mississippi to aid her elderly parents and to serve as
Consultant for Intercultural Awareness for the Jackson Diocese, a position created for her to offer outreach to non-
white communities and to foster interracial awareness, which

[8] Ibid.
[9] Ibid.

expanded her speaking and singing nationally and internationally.

In 1987, the first African American Catholic hymnal, *Lead Me, Guide Me*, was published with significant contributions from Sister Thea.[10] She recorded an album of spirituals in each of the next two years. In 1989 she helped establish the Thea Bowman Black Catholic Educational Foundation to provide scholarships to African American students at Catholic universities.

The year 1984 was one of deep loss for Sister Thea. In November, her mother died at age eighty-one. A month later, her father died at age ninety. It was also the year she began a six-year struggle for her own life. In March, Sister Thea was diagnosed with breast cancer.

She successfully fought the cancer for a year with surgery and treatment and for the next three years continued a full schedule of intercultural advocacy, speaking and singing, and teaching. At the request of the U.S. bishops, she also coordinated and edited a book for ministry to Black Catholics titled *Families: Black and Catholic, Catholic and Black*. In 1988 she learned the cancer, which she had continued to fight, had spread to her bones.

"When I first found out I had cancer, I didn't know if I should pray for healing, or life, or death", she told *Praying* magazine in 1989. "Then I found peace in praying for what my folks call 'God's perfect will.' As it evolved, my prayer has become, *Lord, let me live until I die*. By that I mean I want to live, love and serve fully until death comes."[11]

Sister Thea fulfilled that mission, maintaining an astonishing schedule of ministry for someone in chronic pain

[10] Ibid.
[11] Thea Bowman, *In My Own Words* (Barnhart, Mich.: Liguori Publications, 2009), 102.

with terminal illness until near the end, when she died in her family home the morning of March 30, 1990.

Her grave is next to those of her parents at Elmwood Cemetery in Memphis, Tennessee. In keeping with her Franciscan simplicity, at her request, the inscription on her gravestone humbly states, "She tried." She explained once: "I want people to remember that I tried to love the Lord and that I tried to love them."[12] That she succeeded was well articulated by writer Peter Jesserer Smith who noted: "The disciple tried. The Lord made the saint. What a prophetic witness and testimony for our times."[13] On June 1, 2018, Sister Thea was given the title Servant of God, in the first step toward canonization.

[12] Bowman, *In My Own Words*, 107.
[13] Peter Jesserer Smith, "Bowman: A School of Evangelization and Discipleship", in *Black Catholics on the Road to Sainthood*, ed. Michael R. Heinlein (Huntington, Ind.: Our Sunday Visitor, 2021), 104.

BIBLIOGRAPHY

Chapter 1: Pierre Toussaint

Davis, O.S.B., Cyprian. *The History of Black Catholics in the United States*. Chestnut Ridge, N.Y. Crossroad, 1990.

Jones, Arthur. *Pierre Toussaint: A Biography*. New York: Doubleday, 2003.

Lee, Hannah Farnham Sawyer. *Memoir of Pierre Toussaint: Born a Slave in Santo Domingo*. Boston: Crosby, Nichols, and Company, 1854.

Maillard, Mary. "Pierre Toussaint and Marie-Rose Juliette Gaston". BlackPast.org. Accessed November 8, 2023. blackpast.org/african-american-history/toussaint-pierre -and-juliette/.

O'Connor, Cardinal John. "In the Cathedral Crypt, A Prayer for Haiti". *Catholic New York*, October 21, 1993.

"To Whom Shall We Go?" *Timothy Cardinal Dolan*, August 25, 2010. cardinaldolan.org/blog/to-whom-shall-we -go-13.

Tribunus. "Blessed Pierre Toussaint, the Voluntary Slave Who Confounded the Worldly". *Roman Christendom*, September 5, 2007. romanchristendom.blogspot.com/2007/ 09/blessed-pierre-toussaint-voluntary.html.

"Venerable Pierre Toussaint". Archdiocese of New York. Accessed November 8, 2023. archny.org/ministries-and

-offices/cultural-diversity-apostolate/black-ministry/vene
rable-pierre-toussaint/.

"Venerable Pierre Toussaint, 1766–1853". United States
Conference of Catholic Bishops. Accessed November 8,
2023.   usccb.org/committees/african-american-affairs/road
-sainthood-leaders-african-descent.

"Venerable Pierre Toussaint, 1766–1853, Archdiocese of
New York". *Catechist Café*. Accessed November 8, 2023.
catechistcafe.weebly.com/uploads/9/4/2/8/9428334/saint
s-toussaint.pdf.

Chapter 2: Mary Elizabeth Lange

Catholic News Agency. "Sainthood Cause Advances for
Mother Mary Lange, Educator Who Fought Racism". *National Catholic Register*, December 11, 2019. ncregister.com
/news/sainthood-cause-advances-for-mother-mary-lange
-educator-who-fought-racism.

Davis, O.S.B., Cyprian. *The History of Black Catholics in the
United States*. Chestnut Ridge, N.Y.: Crossroad, 1990.

Gerdes, Reginald. "By Her Works". *What We Have Seen and
Heard: Essays and Stories from Black Catholics of Baltimore*.
Quoted in "Mother Mary Lange". Mother Mary Lange
Guild. Accessed November 8, 2023. motherlange.org/mot
her-lange.

Gerdes, M. Reginald. "To Educate and Evangelize: Black
Catholic Schools of the Oblate Sisters of Providence
(1828–1880)". U.S. Catholic Historian 7, no. 2/3 (Spring-
Summer 1988): 183–99. jstor.org/stable/25153828.

Heinlein, Michael R. "Servant of God Mary Lange". In *Black Catholics on the Road to Sainthood*, edited by Michael R. Heinlein. Huntington, Ind.: Our Sunday Visitor, 2021.

Morrow, Diane Batts. "Outsiders Within: The Oblate Sisters of Providence in the 1830s Church and Society". *U.S. Catholic Historian* 15, no. 2 (Spring 1997): 35–54. jstor.org/stable/25154582.

Morton, Lauren. "Mary Elizabeth Clovis Lange (c. 1784–1882)". Archives of Maryland (Biographical Series), August 24, 2005. msa.maryland.gov/megafile/msa/speccol/sc3500/sc3520/013500/013580/html/13580bio.html.

"Our History". Saint Frances Academy. Accessed November 8, 2023. sfacademy.org/about-us/.

Posey, O.F.M. Cap., Thaddeus J. "Praying in the Shadows: The Oblate Sisters of Providence, a Look at Nineteenth-Century Black Catholic Spirituality". *U.S. Catholic Historian* 12, no. 1 (Winter 1994): 11–30. jstor.org/stable/2515 4009.

Storm, Dean. "Waiting for a Miracle". *Baltimore Magazine*, June 1997. msa.maryland.gov/megafile/msa/speccol/sc35 00/sc3520/013500/013580/pdf/baltjune1997.pdf.

Chapter 3: Cardinal Patrick O'Boyle

"Archbishop Patrick Cardinal O'Boyle Prayer on Civil Rights Act". American Catholic History Classroom. Accessed November 8, 2023. cuomeka.wrlc.org/exhibits/show/the-catholic-church--bishops--/documents/archbishop-patrick-cardinal-o-.

Barnes, Bart. "Cardinal O'Boyle dies at 91". *The Washington Post*, August 11, 1987. washingtonpost.com/archive/politi cs/1987/08/11/cardinal-oboyle-dies-at-91/d8f814ef-ed6b -42e4-b5c9-d7d9c929f440/.

"Biography of Patrick Aloysius Cardinal O'Boyle". Patrick Cardinal O'Boyle Council 11302: Knights of Columbus. Accessed November 8, 2023. oboyle.dcknights.org/index .php/about-us/about-cardinal-o-boyle.

"Former Archbishops of Washington: Patrick A. O'Boyle". Archdiocese of Washington. Accessed November 8, 2023. adw.org/about-us/who-we-are/former-archbishops/.

Jacobe, Stephanie. "The First Cardinal Archbishop of Washington". *Archdiocese of Washington*. Accessed November 8, 2023. adw.org/the-first-cardinal-archbishop-of-washing ton/.

MacGregor, Morris J. *Steadfast in the Faith: The Life of Patrick Cardinal O'Boyle*. Washington, D.C. The Catholic University of America Press, 2006.

O'Boyle, Patrick A. "Invocation by Archbishop Patrick O'Boyle for 1963 March on Washington", August 28, 1963. Lincoln Memorial, Washington, D.C., Archdiocese of Washington. adw.org/invocation-by-archbishop -patrick-oboyle-for-1963-march-on-washington/.

Reagan, Ronald. "Statement on the Death of Patrick Cardinal O'Boyle", August 11, 1987. Ronald Reagan Presidential Library & Museum. reaganlibrary.gov/archives/speech /statement-death-patrick-cardinal-oboyle.

"Statement by Archbishop Patrick A. Cardinal O'Boyle". American Catholic History Classroom. Accessed Novem-

ber 8, 2023. cuomeka.wrlc.org/exhibits/show/the-cathol
ic-church--bishops--/documents/statement-by-archbishop
-patric.

Chapter 4: Mother Henriette Delille

Brett, Edward T. "Race Issues and Conflict in Nineteenth-
and Early Twentieth-Century Religious Life: The New
Orleans Sisters of the Holy Family". *U.S. Catholic Historian* 29, no. 1 (Winter 2011): 113–27. jstor.org/stable/412
89624.

Chatelain, Kim. "The First Real New Orleans Saint? Henriette Delille's Path to Canonization". Nola.com, March 2,
2017. nola.com/archive/article_fdb34525-b68d-5910-9bfe
-931c3acc275d.html.

CNA/EWTN News. "This 18th Century Creole Nun Risked
Her Life to Teach Slaves". *The Catholic Register*, February
20, 2017, catholicregister.org/home/international/item/2
4380-this-18th-century-creole-nun-risked-her-life-to-teac
h-slaves.

"Dates and Events in the Life of Venerable Henriette Delille".
HenrietteDelille.com. Accessed November 8, 2023. henri
ettedelille.com/henriette-delille.

Davis, O.S.B., Cyprian. *The History of Black Catholics in the
United States*. Chestnut Ridge, N.Y.: Crossroad, 1990.

Fessenden, Tracey. "The Sisters of the Holy Family and
the Veil of Race". *Religion and American Culture: A Journal
of Interpretation* 10, no. 2 (Summer 2000): 187–224. jst
or.org/stable/1123946.

Gould, Virginia Meacham, and Charles E. Nolan. "Introduction". In Mary Bernard Deggs, *No Cross, No Crown: Black Nuns in Nineteenth Century New Orleans*, edited by Virginia Meacham Gould and Charles E. Nolan, xxxi–xxxiii. Bloomington, Ind.: Indiana University Press, 2001.

"Healed Aneurysm Investigated as Possible Miracle for Creole Nun's Beatification". Catholic News Agency, August 30, 2019. catholicnewsagency.com/news/42139/healed-aneurysm-investigated-as-possible-miracle-for-creole-nuns-beatification.

Heinlein, Michael. "Venerable Henriette Delille". In *Black Catholics on the Road to Sainthood*, edited by Michael R. Heinlein. Huntington, Ind.: Our Sunday Visitor, 2021.

Johnson, Josh. "Delille: A School of Perseverance and Patience". In *Black Catholics on the Road to Sainthood*, edited by Michael R. Heinlein. Huntington, Ind.: Our Sunday Visitor, 2021.

"Quick Facts: Venerable Henriette's Story". HenrietteDelille.com. Accessed November 8, 2023.

Rector, Theresa A. "Black Nuns as Educators". *The Journal of Negro Education* 51, no. 3 (Summer 1982): 238–53. jstor.org/stable/2294692

Chapter 5: Father Augustus Tolton

Encyclopaedia Britannica Online. S.v. "Augustus Tolton." Accessed July 5, 2023. britannica.com/biography/Augustus-Tolton.

Burke-Sivers, Harold. *Father Augustus Tolton: The Slave Who Became the First African American Priest.* Birmingham, Ala.: EWTN Publishing, Inc., 2018.

Davis, O.S.B., Cyprian. *The History of Black Catholics in the United States.* Chestnut Ridge, N.Y.: Crossroad, 1991.

"Fr. Tolton's Life and Times". Archdiocese of Chicago. Accessed November 8, 2023. tolton.archchicago.org/about/life-and-times.

Hemesath, Caroline. *From Slave to Priest: The Inspirational Story of Father Augustine Tolton (1854–1897).* San Francisco: Ignatius Press, 2006.

Perry, Joseph. "Father Augustus Tolton, 1854–1897". Archdiocese of Chicago. Accessed November 8, 2023. tolton.archchicago.org/documents/1604561/1604725/Tolton+Biography+-+PDF/d8d2f8ac-b0c6-4180-b474-0ea68b4849ba.

Chapter 6: Diane Nash

Biden, Joe. "Remarks by President Biden at Presentation of the Presidential Medal of Freedom". The White House, Washington, D.C., July 7, 2022. The White House. whitehouse.gov/briefing-room/speeches-remarks/2022/07/07/remarks-by-president-biden-at-presentation-of-the-presidential-medal-of-freedom/.

Bliss, Jessica. "On April 19, 1960, the Bombing of a Civil Rights Attorney's Home Set Off a Protest like Few Had Seen in Nashville". *The (Nashville) Tennessean*, April 18, 2020. tennessean.com/story/news/politics/2020/04/19/n

ashville-civil-rights-protest-april-1960-after-lawyer-z-ale
xander-looby-bombing/4807161002/.

"Diane Nash". Iowa State University: Archives of Women's
Political Communication. Accessed November 8, 2023.
awpc.cattcenter.iastate.edu/directory/diane-nash/.

Eyes on the Prize: America's Civil Rights Years (1954–1965).
Documentary series produced by Blackside, Inc., 1987,
transcript. PBS: American Experience.

Freedom Riders. 2011 documentary by American Experience.
Transcript. *PBS: American Experience*. pbs.org/wgbh/amer
icanexperience/films/freedomriders/#transcript.

Morgan, Thaddeus. "How Freedom Rider Diane Nash Risked
Her Life to Desegregate the South". History, March 8,
2018, updated January 27, 2021. history.com/news/diane
-nash-freedom-rider-civil-rights-movement.

Nash, Diane. "Address to the National Catholic Conference
for Interracial Justice". August 25, 1961, Detroit, Michigan. Iowa State University: Archives of Women's Political
Communication. awpc.cattcenter.iastate.edu/2019/08/09/
address-to-the-national-catholic-conference-for-interracial
-justice-august-25-1961/.

Olson, Lynne. *Freedom's Daughters: The Unsung Heroines of
the Civil Rights Movement from 1830–1970*. New York: Scribner, 2001. archive.org/details/freedomsdaughter000olso.

Worthen, Meredith. "Diane Nash Biography". Biography,
July 9, 2020. biography.com/activist/diane-nash. See also
Olson, *Freedom's Daughters*, 153.

Chapter 7: Julia Greeley

Burkey, O.F.M. Cap., Blaine, ed. *In Secret Service of the Sacred Heart: Life and Virtues of Julia Greeley*. 3rd expanded ed. Denver: Julia Greeley Guild, 2021.

"Highest Honor Ever Paid to Dead Laic Here Goes to Negress". *Denver Catholic Register*, June 13, 1918. archives .archden.org/islandora/object/archden%3A2859/datastre am/OBJ/view.

Hying, Donald J. "Understanding the Devotion to the Sacred Heart of Jesus and What it Means". *Simply Catholic*. Accessed November 8, 2023. simplycatholic.com/why -the-sacred-heart/.

Noel, Tom. "Noel: Julia Greeley, 'Angel of Charity.'" *The Denver Post*, February 14, 2014, denverpost.com/2014/02/ 14/noel-julia-greeley-angel-of-charity/.

Chapter 8: Nicholas Black Elk

Costello, Damian. *Black Elk: Colonialism and Lakota Catholicism*. Maryknoll, N.Y.: Orbis Books, 2005.

Costello, Damian. "Nicholas Black Elk: Prophet to Lakota a sign of hope today". *CatholicPhilly.com*, April 15, 2019. catholicphilly.com/2019/04/commentaries/nicholas-black -elk-prophet-to-lakota-a-sign-of-hope-today/.

Gruss, Robert D. "Homily for the Mass Concluding the Diocesan Phase of the Cause for Beatification and Canonization of Servant of God Nicholas William Black Elk, Sr." Saint Agnes Church, Manderson, S.D. BlackElkCan onization.com, June 25, 2019. blackelkcanonization.com

/wp-content/uploads/2019/10/Mass-for-the-Conclusion -of-the-Diocesan-Phase-of-the-Cause-for-Beatification-an d-Canonization-of-Servant-of-God-Nicholas-W.pdf.

Hallstrom, Laurie. "Black Elk, Cause for Canonization to Open". *West River Catholic*, October 2017. rapidcitydio cese.org/wp-content/uploads/2017/10/WRC-oct-17-redu ced.pdf.

McNamara, Patrick. "Nicholas Black Elk: This Sioux Medi- cine Man May Be Recognized as a Saint". *Aleteia*, Novem- ber 17, 2017. aleteia.org/2017/11/16/nicholas-black-elk -this-sioux-medicine-man-may-be-recognized-as-a-saint/.

Smith, Peter Jesserer. "Black Elk: Future Patron Saint and Model for Instituted Lay Catechists?". *National Catho- lic Register*, August 18, 2021. ncregister.com/news/black -elk-future-patron-saint-and-model-for-instituted-lay-cate chists.

Steltenkamp, Michael F. *Nicholas Black Elk: Medicine Man, Missionary, Mystic*. Norman, Okla.: University of Okla- homa Press, 2009.

Chapter 9: Saint Teresa of Calcutta

Egan, Eileen. *Prayertimes with Mother Teresa*. New York: Im- age Books, 1989.

———. *Such a Vision of the Street: Mother Teresa, The Spirit and the Work*. London: Sidgwick & Jackson, 1986.

Kolodiejchuk, M.C., Brian, ed. *Mother Teresa: Come Be My Light*. New York: Doubleday, 2007.

Martin, S.J., James. "Teresa of Jesus". In *Mother Teresa: The Life and Works of a Modern Saint*, edited by Richard Lacayo. New York: Time Books, 2012.

"Mother Teresa Biography". Biography.com, updated February 24, 2020. biography.com/religious-figures/mother-teresa.

"Mother Teresa of Calcutta (1910–1997)". The Holy See. Accessed November 9, 2023. vatican.va/news_services/liturgy/saints/ns_lit_doc_20031019_madre-teresa_en.html.

Muggeridge, Malcolm. *Something Beautiful for God*. New York: Ballantine Books, 1971.

Nicol, Mike. "Mother Teresa". *Love: The Words and Inspiration of Mother Teresa*. Boulder: Blue Mountain Press, 2007.

Nobel Prize, The. "The Nobel Peace Prize 1979". Press release, October 27, 1979. nobelprize.org/prizes/peace/1979/press-release/.

Spink, Kathryn. *Mother Teresa: A Complete Authorized Biography*. San Francisco: HarperSanFrancisco, 1997.

Tighe, Tommy. "Dorothy Day, Mother Teresa and the 5-Finger Gospel". *Aleteia,* April 21, 2017. aleteia.org/2017/04/21/dorothy-day-mother-teresa-and-the-5-finger-gospel/.

Van Biema, David. "Her Agony". In *Mother Teresa: The Life and Works of a Modern Saint*, edited by Richard Lacayo. New York: Time Books, 2012.

Vogt, Brandon. "Jesus in His Most Distressing Disguise". Word on Fire, September 5, 2014. wordonfire.org/articles/jesus-in-his-most-distressing-disguise/.

Chapter 10: Sister Norma Pimentel

Dart, Tom. "Child Migrants at Texas Border: An Immigration Crisis That's Hardly New". *The Guardian*, July 9, 2014. theguardian.com/world/2014/jul/09/us-immigration-undocumented-children-texas.

Gramlich, John. "Migrant Encounters at U.S.-Mexico Border Are at a 21-Year High." Pew Research Center, August 13, 2021. pewresearch.org/fact-tank/2021/08/13/migrant-encounters-at-u-s-mexico-border-are-at-a-21-year-high/.

Gramlich, John, and Alissa Scheller. "What's Happening at the U.S.-Mexico Border in 7 Charts". Pew Research Center, November 9, 2021. pewresearch.org/fact-tank/2021/11/09/whats-happening-at-the-u-s-mexico-border-in-7-charts/.

Greenblatt, Alan. "What's Causing the Latest Immigration Crisis? A Brief Explainer". *NPR*, July 9, 2014. npr.org/2014/07/09/329848538/whats-causing-the-latest-immigration-crisis-a-brief-explainer.

Lind, Dara. "The 2014 Central American Migrant Crisis". *Vox*, October 10, 2014. vox.com/2014/10/10/18088638/child-migrant-crisis-unaccompanied-alien-children-rio-grande-valley-obama-immigration.

"'Migrant Protection Protocols': Fact Sheet, The". American Immigration Council, January 7, 2022. americanimmigrationcouncil.org/research/migrant-protection-protocols.

Pimentel, M.J., Sr. Norma. "Opinion: What Biden Can Do for Migrants Stuck in Mexico, Despite MPP". *The Washington Post*, September 6, 2021, washingtonpost.com/opini

ons/2021/09/06/norma-pimentel-mpp-biden-help-migran
ts/.

————. Testimony to U.S. Commission on Civil Rights,
2014. U.S. Commission on Civil Rights. Accessed November 9, 2023. usccr.gov/files/pubs/OIG/Sr._Norma_
Pimentel's_130.15_TestimonyUSCommisionCivilRights
.pdf.

Salgado, Soli, and Dan Stockman. "Sr. Norma Pimentel,
LCWR Award Recipient, Embraces 'Holy Chaos' of Her
Ministry to Migrants". *Global Sisters Report*, August 17,
2019. globalsistersreport.org/news/ministry-trends/sr-no
rma-pimentel-lcwr-award-recipient-embraces-holy-chaos
-her-ministry.

Chapter 11: Saint Katharine Drexel

Baldwin, Lou. *A Call to Sanctity: The Formation and Life of
Mother Katharine Drexel*. Philadelphia: The Catholic Standard and Times, 1988.

Chervin, Ronda De Sola. *Treasury of Women Saints*. Ann Arbor, Mich.: Servant Publications, 1991.

Ellsberg, Robert. *All Saints: Daily Reflections on Saints, Prophets, and Witnesses for Our Time*. Chestnut Ridge, N.Y.:
Crossroad Publishing, 1998.

Fink, John F. "Saint Katharine Drexel". *American Saints: Five
Centuries of Heroic Sanctity on the American Continents*. New
York: Alba House, 2001.

"Founding of the Sisters of the Blessed Sacrament". Saint
Katharine Drexel Shrine. Accessed November 19, 2023.
saintkatharinedrexelshrine.com/founding-of-the-sisters/.

Hughes, Cheryl C.D. *Katharine Drexel: The Riches-to-Rags Story of an American Catholic Saint*. Grand Rapids, Mich.: Eerdmans Publishing Co., 2014.

John Paul II, Pope. Homily at the Canonization Mass of Katharine Drexel (October 1, 2000). vatican.va/content/j ohn-paul-ii/en/homilies/2000/documents/hf_jp-ii_hom_2 0001001_canonization.pdf.

"Katharine Drexel: 1858–1955". The Holy See. Accessed November 10, 2023. vatican.va/news_services/liturgy/sai nts/ns_lit_doc_20001001_katharine-drexel_en.html.

Murray, Cecilia. "Katharine Drexel: Learning to Love the Poor". *Catholic Education: A Journal of Inquiry and Practice*, 9, no. 3 (March 2006): 307–19. files.eric.ed.gov/fulltext/ EJ1006058.pdf.

"Saint Katharine Drexel: The Heart of a Woman, the Strength of a Saint". Saint Katharine Drexel Shrine. saintkatharine drexelshrine.com/about/.

Tarry, Ellen. *Katharine Drexel: Friend of the Neglected*. New York: Vision, 1958.

Chapter 12: Saint Oscar Romero

Brockman, James R. *Romero: A Life*. Maryknoll, N.Y.: Orbis Books, 1990.

"The Century of Romero: 1917–2017". Archbishop Romero Trust. Accessed March 20, 2024. romerotrust.org.uk/sites /default/files/documents/Century%20of%20Romero%20 2018%20update.pdf.

Clarke, Kevin. *Oscar Romero: Love Must Win Out*. Collegeville, Minn.: Liturgical Press, 2014.

Dada, Carlos. "Así matamos a monseñor Romero". *El Faro*, March 25, 2010. elfaro.net/es/201003/noticias/1403/.

Ellsberg, Robert. *All Saints: Daily Reflections on Saints, Prophets, and Witnesses for Our Time*. New York: Crossroad Publishing, 1997.

Encyclopaedia Britannica Online. S.v. "St. Óscar Romero". Accessed March 20, 2024. britannica.com/biography/Oscar-Arnulfo-Romero

Francis, Pope. Homily at the Canonization Mass for Oscar Romero. October 14, 2018. vatican.va/content/francesco/en/homilies/2018/documents/papa-francesco_2018 1014_omelia-canonizzazione.html.

Francis, Pope. Letter to the Archbishop of San Salvador for the Beatification of Oscar Romero. May 23, 2015. vatican.va/content/francesco/en/letters/2015/documents/papa-francesco_20150523_lettera-beatificazione-romero.html.

Kellogg Institute for International Studies. "Archbishop Oscar Romero". Kellogg Institute for International Studies, University of Notre Dame. Accessed March 20, 2024. kellogg.nd.edu/archbishop-oscar-romero.

Lovett, Sean-Patrick. "Remembering St. Oscar Romero: 40 Years after His Assassination". Vatican News. March 24, 2020. vaticannews.va/en/church/news/2020-03/oscar-romero-forty-years-assassination-anniversary0.html.

Morozzo Della Rocca, Roberto. *Oscar Romero: Prophet of Hope*. London: Darton, Longman & Todd, 2015.

"Salvador Archbishop Assassinated by Sniper While Officiating at Mass." *New York Times*, March 25, 1980. nytimes
.com/1980/03/25/archives/salvador-archbishop-assassinat
ed-by-sniper-while-officiating-at.html.

"Who Was Romero?" Archbishop Romero Trust. Accessed
March 20, 2024. romerotrust.org.uk/who-was-romero.

Chapter 13: Paul and Pat Bokulich

Bokulich, Paul, and Pat Bokulich. "SCLC, 1965–1968, Alabama, Georgia, South Carolina." First person account,
2007. Civil Rights Movement Archive. Accessed November 10, 2023, crmvet.org/vet/bokulich.htm.

Bokulich v. Jury Commission 394 U.S. 97 (1969).

"Courthouse Square Dedication to Former Sheriff Thomas
E. Gilmore Held This Past Saturday". *Washington Informer*,
October 22, 2013. washingtoninformer.com/courthouse
-square-dedication-to-former-sheriff-thomas-e-gilmore-he
ld-this-past-saturday/.

"Effect of the Voting Rights Act, The." U.S. Department of
Justice, updated August 6, 2015. justice.gov/crt/introducti
on-federal-voting-rights-laws-0.

Guzman, Isaiah, and Santa Cruz Sentinel. "Soquel Man
Recalls His Place in Civil Rights Fight: Paul Bokulich
Worked under Martin Luther King Jr". *Santa Cruz Sentinel*, February 29, 2012. santacruzsentinel.com/2012/02/
29/soquel-man-recalls-his-place-in-civil-rights-fight-paul-b
okulich-worked-under-martin-luther-king-jr/.

Harmon, Catherine. "A Catholic Looks Back on His Time
in the Civil Rights Movement." *The Catholic World Report*,

January 20, 2020. catholicworldreport.com/2020/01/20/a
-catholic-looks-back-on-his-time-in-the-civil-rights-move
ment/.

Kass, Amy A., and Leon R. Kass, eds. *The Meaning of Martin
Luther King Jr. Day.* Washington, D.C.: What So Proudly
We Hail, 2013. aei.org/wp-content/uploads/2013/01/-mlk
-bookforweb1_160442341689.pdf.

Merrill, Linda, Lisa Rogers, and Kaye Passmore. *Picturing
America: Teachers Resource Book.* Edited by Carol Peters.
Washington, D.C.: National Endowment for the Humanities, 2008. picturingamerica.neh.gov/downloads/pdfs/R
esource_Guide_Chapters/PictAmer_Resource_Book_Cha
pter_19B.pdf.

Murray, Paul. "Selma March at 50: 54-Mile Trek Was 'Magnificent'". *National Catholic Reporter*, March 10, 2015.
ncronline.org/blogs/ncr-today/selma-march-50-54-mile-tr
ek-was-magnificent.

"Patricia Ann Bokulich". Obituary. *Santa Cruz Sentinel*,
March 31, 2012. legacy.com/us/obituaries/santacruzsenti
nel/name/patricia-bokulich-obituary?pid=156775096.

"Selma to Montgomery March". The Martin Luther King
Jr. Research and Education Institute. Stanford University.
Accessed November 11, 2023. kinginstitute.stanford.edu/
encyclopedia/selma-montgomery-march.

"U.S. Judge Blocks Grand Jury Action." *The Southern Courier*, October 1–2, 1966. crmvet.org/docs/sc/sc661001
.pdf.

You Have to Have Light to Dispel Darkness. Sean Schiavolin, director, cinematographer, and editor. 2020. YouTube video. youtube.com/watch?v=wFaLSQmRNJc&t=37s.

Chapter 14: Dorothy Day

Allaire, James, and Rosemary Broughton. "An Introduction to the Life and Spirituality of Dorothy Day". Excerpt from *Praying with Dorothy Day: Companions for the Journey.* Winona, Minn.: St. Mary's Press, 1995. catholicworker.org/life-and-spirituality-dorothy-day/.

Day, Dorothy. *The Long Loneliness: An Autobiography.* New York: Harper & Row, 1952.

———. "Peter Maurin". *Catholic Worker,* May 1977. catholicworker.org/dorothyday/articles/256.html.

"Directory of Catholic Worker Communities". Catholic Worker Movement. Accessed November 13, 2022. catholicworker.org/communities/directory-picker.html.

Forest, Jim. *All is Grace: A Biography of Dorothy Day.* Maryknoll, N.Y.: Orbis Books, 2011.

———. "Biography of Peter Maurin". Catholic Worker Movement, February 11, 2022. catholicworker.org/petermaurin/pm-biography.html.

Francis, Pope. Visit to the Joint Session of the United States Congress (Washington, D.C. September 24, 2015). vatican.va/content/francesco/en/speeches/2015/september/documents/papa-francesco_20150924_usa-us-congress.html.

"Thirty Interesting Facts about Dorothy Day's Life". Catholic Worker Movement, February 11, 2022. catholicworker .org/dorothyday/dd-interesting-facts.html.

Zablotny, Carolyn. "A Woman of Conscience." Dorothy Day Guild, 2023. dorothydayguild.org/a-woman-of-cons cience/.

————. "Movement to Canonize Dorothy Day". Dorothy Day Guild, 2023. dorothydayguild.org/timeline/move ment-to-canonize-dorothy-day.

Chapter 15: Blessed Franz Jägerstätter

"Bl. Franz Jägerstätter (1907–1943): Layman and Martyr". The Holy See. Accessed November 14, 2023. vatican.va/ news_services/liturgy/saints/ns_lit_doc_20071026_jagerst atter_en.html.

Forest, Jim. "Introduction". In *Franz Jägerstätter: Letters and Writings from Prison*, edited by Erna Putz. Maryknoll, N.Y.: Orbis Books, 2009.

"Franz Jägerstätter 1907–1943, Martyr, Short Biography". Linz Diocese. Accessed November 14, 2023. dioezese -linz.at/site/jaegerstaetter/english/biography/article/2252 8.html.

Hallock, Daniel. "Franz Jägerstätter, A Quiet Martyr." *Plough*, May 28, 2019. plough.com/en/topics/justice/nonviolence /franz-jagerstatter-a-quiet-martyr.

Merton, Thomas. *Faith and Violence: Christian Teaching and Christian Practice*. Notre Dame, Ind.: University of Notre Dame Press, 1968.

Miller, Michael. "Previously Unknown Document by Blessed Franz Jägerstätter Discovered". *The Catholic World Report,* June 5, 2022. catholicworldreport.com/2022/06/05/previously-unknown-document-by-blessed-franz-jagerstatter-discovered/.

Warde, Samuel. "Franz Jägerstätter Chose the Guillotine Over Pledging Loyalty to Hitler". *All That's Interesting,* December 24, 2019, updated Jan. 2, 2020. allthatsinteresting.com/franz-jagerstatter.

Wicker, Brian. "The Significance of Franz Jägerstätter". *New Blackfriars* 89, no. 1022 (July 2008): 385–88. jstor.org/stable/43251244.

Zahn, Gordon. *In Solitary Witness: The Life and Death of Franz Jägerstätter.* New York: Beacon Press, 1964.

Chapter 16: Sister Thea Bowman

Bowman, Thea. *In My Own Words.* Barnhart, Mich.: Liguori, 2009.

———. "Sr. Thea Bowman's Address to the U.S. Bishop's Conference June 1989". usccb.org/issues-and-action/cultural-diversity/african-american/resources/upload/Transcript-Sr-Thea-Bowman-June-1989-Address.pdf.

Nutt, Maurice J. *Thea Bowman: Faithful and Free.* Collegeville, Minn.: Liturgical Press, 2019.

Smith, Charlene, and John Feister. *Thea's Song: The Life of Thea Bowman.* Maryknoll, N.Y.: Orbis Books, 2009. Kindle.

Smith, Peter Jesserer. "Bowman: A School of Evangelization and Discipleship." In *Black Catholics on the Road to Sainthood*, edited by Michael R. Heinlein. Huntington, Ind.: Our Sunday Visitor, 2021.

Szczepanowski, Richard. "Catholic University Names Street in Honor of Sister Thea Bowman". *Catholic News Service*, May 2, 2022. catholicnews.com/catholic-university-names-street-in-honor-of-sister-thea-bowman/.